© 2002 Feierabend Verlag OHG
Mommsenstrasse 43, D-10629 Berlin

Editorial project:

LOFT Publications
Domènech, 9 2-2
08012 Barcelona, Spain
e-mail: loft@loftpublications.com

Editorial coordination: Cynthia Reschke
Art director: Mireia Casanovas Soley
Grafic Design: Sheila Bonet

Concept: Paco Asensio, Peter Feierabend

Printing and binding: Stige, Turin

Printed in Italy
ISBN 3-936761-50-7
61 06007 1

The big book of
RESIDENTIALS

Feierabend

The Big Book of Residentials

Introduction

The residence has evolved gradually over time. Originally their sole purpose was to provide warmth and shelter, but now they have come to symbolize something far more personal.

The home represents our tastes, values and even our personalities. This phenomenon, aided by architects around the world, has become evident in the residences which people live in today. Single family houses, residential buildings, apartments, lofts and studios are some of the most common living spaces, which come in a variety of sizes, shapes and styles to suit their particular tenants. The Big Book of Residentials is just that, a big book that features over 100 different projects by the best international contemporary architects around. The book is divided into chapters by types: single family homes, multiresidential buildings, apartments, and unfinsihed projects. Each of these sections is broken down further into styles, categories or types, exhibiting many examples and granting a multitude of ideas for those looking to build a new home, architects or those who are simply interested in architecture. Contemporary, classical, or rustic interiors, cabins and prefabricated structures. Private residences and social housing. Small studios, apartments, lofts. Projects in the stages of evolution that are yet to be materialized. Full-color photographs, plans, drawings and descriptive texts accompany and illustrate each project, aiding the reader through this stunning and comprehensive collection of international residences.

Single Family Dwellings

This sections aims to represent different kinds
of single family residences that exist today. The styles
vary anywhere from modern and contemporary.
to classial. to rustic and not only in the form of
conventional structures but also in the form of cabins
and homes made out of prefabricated materials.

Tagomago house
Carlos Ferrater ○ Joan Guibernau

This house overlooks the sea on the island of Tagomago in Ibiza, Spain. A family vacation home, the residence is organized around a principal nucleus and a series of small structures or pavilions that enjoy a certain autonomy. The building is organized across a longitudinal axis that links all the rooms with the nucleus, offering isolated and independent areas that enjoy an optimal orientation. In addition, the composition of distinct, isolated volumes created a series of open spaces that form patios, porches and terraces, linking interior and exterior.

The living room opens onto a large wooden terrace overlooking the pool, flanked by a large canopy of reinforced concrete. The rooms that make up the nucleus of the house include a hallway, living room, dining room, kitchen, services and master bedroom with bath. A guest room features a terrace solarium above it. A patio separates the central volume from the four small pavilions for the children.

The architects used traditional materials for the construction that are typical of the region, such as stone for the façades and walls and wood for the carpentry and terrace floors. The partitions are traditional and are made out of concrete beams and small ceramic vaults. In the living room, a large continuous window protects it from the sun with an eave that crosses its entire length to offer a wide view of the surroundings and to communicate the interior with the terrace and the pool.

Architects: **Carlos Ferrater and Joan Guibernau**
Location: **San Carlos. Ibiza. Spain**
Area: **8.065 sq.feet**
Construction date: **2001**
Photographs: **Alejo Bagué**

The rectilinear forms that make up this complex of simple, austere volumes emphasize the materials: the white stone and concrete contrast with the dark wood of the terrace.

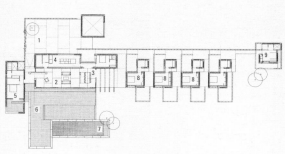

Plant

1. Entrance - 2. Living room - 3. Dining room -
4. Kitchen - 5. Main bedroom - 6. Terrace
7. Swimming pool -8. Bedrooms - 9. Guest
room

The pool, situated in front of the living room, is surrounded by a wooden platform that overlooks the surrounding view. A large portico is placed between the two spaces, creating a covered exterior zone that also filters the light that shines inside.

The architectural language of the house, even though it has a solid and contemporary character, respects the island's traditional architecture by using local materials, including stone and wood.

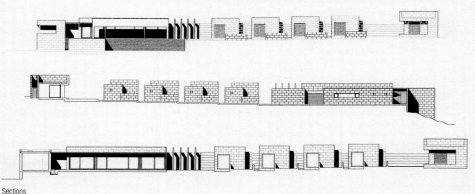

Sections

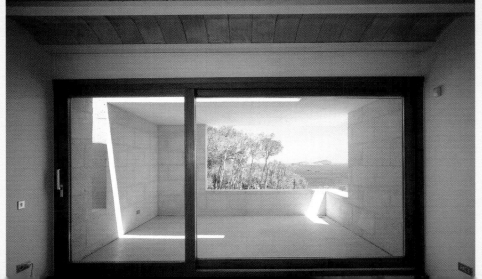

The layout of the walls generates openings towards the exterior. Large windows framed in natural-colored wood stretch from one extreme to the other.

divides the dining room from the living room.

Reyna Residence

Dean Nota Architect

This house is located on a 30 x 79-foot lot situated on the marine front of Hermosa Beach, a coastal settlement in the western part of the Los Angeles metropolitan area. The setting's dominant physical characteristic is the views of the beach and the ocean framed by a pier in the north, and of the Palos Verdes Peninsula and Santa Catalina Island in the south. Hermosa Beach is an environment in transition, which mixes small, older structures with contemporary architectural structures of a bigger scale.

The client required a residence for one or two people and occasional guests. The idea was to provide access to the public life and social interaction of the pedestrian walkway, while creating a more private ambience for entertainment and rest. The layout is thus organized on three levels, which ascend toward the most private space. A guest room, family room and parking are located on the ground floor next to the double entrance. The living room, dining room, kitchen and a second bedroom occupy the two intermediate levels, while the master bedroom and bathroom are located on the top floor to take advantage of the best views.

A modest and austere entrance leads to a spatial experience that expands in a sequence articulated by the stairway, which connects the different areas of house. The arrival at each level reveals a space that opens progressively to the light and the ocean views. Each one of the three floors extends to the exterior with terraces that overlook the oceanfront.

Architect: Dean Nota Architect AIA
Collaborators: Stephen Billings, Josep Fedorowich, Marina Mizruh (interior design)
Location: Hermosa Beach, California, United States
Area: 3,440 sq.feet
Construction date: 2000
Photographs: Erhard Pfeiffer

On the eastern façade, the house is presented as a closed and solid volume. On the front facing the beach, it appears as a completely transparent object open to the sea. The house's solid materials contrast with the lightness of the roof and the inclined form of the back façade.

The balconies, enormous pieces that lean towards the ocean, seem to float in the middle of the large glass façade on the back part of the house. The juxtaposition of exterior spaces, the interior walkway and the large window endow the interior with spatial richness.

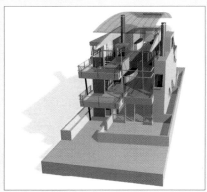

3-D Model

The heart of the house is a large space that contains the living areas and is directly related to the beach by way of a large glass surface.

1. Entrance - 2. Parking - 3. Living room
4. Bedrooms - 5. Terrace
6. Living room - 7. Dining room - 8. Kitchen
9. Main bedroom - 10. Terrace

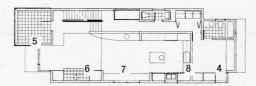

Second floor

First floor

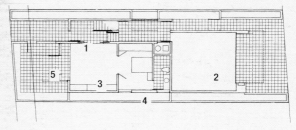

Ground floor

Section and elevation

B House

Barclay·Crousse Architects

This project began with an analysis of the environment surrounding the site. Even though the land is located in one of the most arid deserts of the world, its climatic conditions are not extreme. The challenge was to create a totally permeable architecture in which the walls emphasize the landscape and provide just enough privacy to make the building habitable.

Building the house on such a steep hillside made it possible to open only one façade to the exterior. The next step was to separate the walls in order to create different ways of relating them to the sea landscape and to make the most of the only view. The house is divided into three levels, united by an exterior stairway. A social area separates the parent's level on the upper floor from the children's quarters on the lower level.

The staircase is the axis that structures the project, as well as the element that unites the distinct levels of the house with one another and the beach. Its configuration reveals the slope of the land and frames the view towards the sea. The house is entered from the top of the hill, at the roof, where a platform also serves as a parking area.

Each level has a specific complementary activity that relates to a vertical wall and connects it in a distinct manner with the landscape. For example, the parents' level has a more intimate exterior zone, and the children's level includes a television room in which the wall serves as blinds that diffuse the intensity of the light.

Architect: Sandra Barclay and Jean Pierre Crousse
Collaborators: Carlos Casabone (structure)
Location: The Escondida beach, Cañete, Peru
Area: 2,839 sq. feet
Construction date: 1999
Photographs: Roberto Huarcaya

This project arose from a reflection on three essential factors: the climatic conditions of the Peruvian coast, the geographic conditions of the site and the special needs of the client.

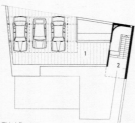

Third floor

Second floor

First floor

Ground floor

1. Parking - 2. Entrance - 3. Main room
4. Guest room - 5. Kitchen - 6. Dining room
7. Terrace - 8. Living - 9. Bedrooms

This house's spectacular geographic location was a challenge for the architects who strove to make the most of the surrounding landscape. The building is embedded in half of the slope, emphasizing the project's direction towards the ocean view.

As an object that hangs down from the high part of the slope, the building is vertical, with multiple spatial relationships between the different levels and the sea. A series of terraces, solariums and exterior zones develop towards the beach.

Section

Elevation

Location plan

The clarity and force of the scheme created clear and luminous spaces that frame the view from different perspectives. While strong colors are used on the exterior to contrast with the monochromatic landscape, the interior features a range of whites that create a fresh, relaxed atmosphere.

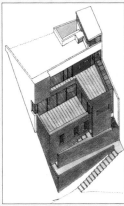

Axonometry

M House

Brian MacKay-Lyons

As a house in the desert, this building had to create an intimate space amidst a vast landscape. On the other hand, the presence of the ocean called for the house to open up towards the horizon. The architectural plans started with this contradiction: to establish a dialectical relationship between closure and opening, opacity and transparency, intimacy and exteriority, tradition and modernity.

The simple, closed volumes form a composition of masses that integrate with the abstract desert landscape. Following local building traditions, the architects first established a site and then demarcated the land with walls that preserve the intimacy of the exterior zones, while relating them to the interior space of the house.

The house is divided into three areas that contain its different functions. The first consists of parking and the entrance. The children's bedrooms and the guest quarters occupy the central volume, while the parent's bedroom — situated above the living room, dining room and kitchen — makes up the third.

Imbalances permit the residents to perceive the ocean from even the most remote spots. The limits between the interior and exterior façade are due to the use of light and transparency, un-framed glass, and to the treatment of the materials. The sequence first leads to an elongated patio that follows the slope of the land with a soft staircase. The path then leads to a terrace, where there is a pool, in the form of the balcony, above the cliff and the sea.

Architect: Sandra Barclay and Jean Pierre Crousse
Collaborators: Carlos Casabone (structure)
Location: The Escondida beach, Cañete, Peru
Area: 1,185 sq. feet
Construction: 2001
Photographs: Jean Pierre Crousse

This project resulted from a meditation on the dichotomy of building on the Peruvian coast, which mixes two distinct landscapes: the arid desert and a view of the sea.

The project's play of volumes creates various scenarios in which the sea is ever-present and framed by architectural elements like porticos and large windows. The chromatic play complements this diversity and contrasts with the surroundings.

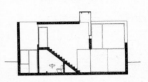

Transverse section

Longitudinal section

Longitudinal section

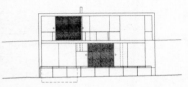

Longitudinal section

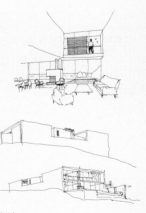

Sketches

1. Parking - 2. Entrance
3. Bedrooms - 4. Main room
5. Living room/Dining room - 6. Kitchen
7. Terrace - 8. Swimming pool

First floor

Ground floor

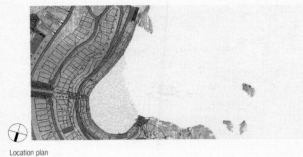

In contrast to the solid materials with which the house is built, elements like glass, wooden platforms and blinds offer a counterpoint of lightness, linking the project to the regional architecture.

Light House

Lehrer Architects

This residence in Capistrano Beach makes the most of its surroundings and the available surface area. The interior features so much glass and light that the walls seem nonexistent and the materials seem to disappear. The architectural challenge was to maximize the space, the presence of the beach and the spectacular views of the landscape.

The architect's solution was to create a large, curved wall, which is used as a reference throughout the project. The public zone gradually becomes related —as the volume develops— to the exterior and to the beach. The different spaces that make up the residence's design are grouped along the curved wall, which contains openings and glass boxes that house each area. The transparency of the spaces emphasizes the views, links the spaces to one another, and highlights the presence of the curved wall throughout the house.

Despite the site's minimal proportions, especially in terms of width, the architect created interesting areas and paths. The main entrance is located along a lateral patio, creating an extended entrance protected by a portico. The volume suspended from the master bedroom has windows on all four sides. Ocean views and the presence of geometry in the project give this house a unique character.

Lighting was strategically placed to take advantage of the quality of natural light and to emphasize the architectural elements. As a result, this project of multiple spatial relationships continually offers new antidotes to discover.

Architect: Michael B. Lehrer
Location: Capistrano Beach, California.
United States
Area: 4,731 sq. feet
Construction date: 1997
Photographs: Michael Arden

An intricate, volumetric design makes the most of the lot's narrow proportions and creates transparencies and visual relationships between the different spaces and the exterior.

The rigid and elongated form of the property breaks because of a geometry that creates diverse situations in the surroundings as well as different spatial relationships in the interior. The circulation and living areas have visual contact with the rest of the house.

1. Entrance - 2. Living room - 3. Terrace
4. Dining room - 5. Kitchen - 6. Studio
7. Parking - 8. Main room - 9. Bathroom
10. Bedrooms

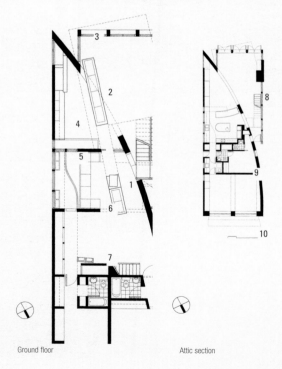

Ground floor

Attic section

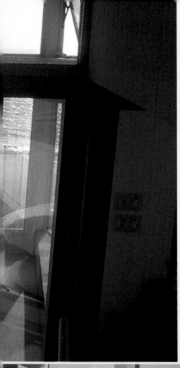

The square frames of the exterior windows are repeated inside the residence as divisions of the different areas. The partitions frame each zone and create an interesting optical effect that makes the most of the beach views.

Elevations

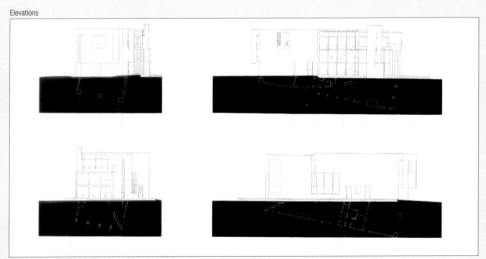

Winer Residence

Stelle Architects

This project started with an old 214 square-foot house, that over time had become surrounded by much larger buildings with a greater presence in the landscape. In order to amplify the summer residence and make it appropriate for the needs of a larger family, the architect added on a 362- square- foot structure.

The addition provided more living and sleeping areas while maintaining privacy and the ambience of a small house. The new building was designed to follow its previous layout, architecture and details. In an attempt to respect the original structure as much as possible, the architect built a transparent structure that serves as the entrance and as the nexus between the old part and the new. Its transparency contrasts with the solidity of the front façades and permits a view of the sea across the entrance. A series of piles i and a wooden platform raise the building off the ground. A linear window runs along the façade and separates the roof from the principal volume.

After entering the house, the visitor finds the sequence of the kitchen, living room, bathroom and bedroom. Towards the view of the beach, a continual and transparent façade crosses all the spaces, creating the sensation of a unique and continual space. The materials that the architect used agree with the environmental conditions and are mostly typical of the coast and tolerant of the climate. Principal elements feature painted cedar, stainless steel, the color mahogany, copper covered in lead and glass.

Architect: Stelle Architects
Collaborators: Kate Evarts, Frederick Stelle, Conny Renner, Walter Enkerli, Verena Olson, Grayson Jordan, Jonathan Tyler, Alex Keller, Eleanor Donnelly
Location: Bridgehampton, United States
Area: 1,205 sq. feet
Construction date: 2001
Photographs: Jeff Heatley

The project, a basic, longitudinal volume, is set into the landscape with great subtlety. The addition also respects the original character of the house to which it is attached.

Location plan

The new construction uses as a reference –in terms of formal language and structural system– the old house that occupied the lot and to which the new one is attached. The addition is lightly separated from the original building, yet the two are united by a wooden roof, which respects the existing architecture.

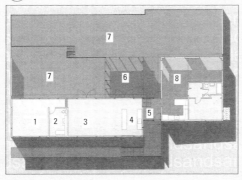

1. Bedroom - 2. Bathroom

3. Living room/Dining room - 4. Kitchen

5. Entrance - 6. Corridor - 7. Terrace

8. Original house

Plan

The continuous glass façade towards the northeast links the spaces of the new construction and relates them closely to the exterior terraces and gallery, which are like extensions of the interior. The view of the sea is the space's real boundary.

In the bathroom and in the kitchen, the furnishings and appliances are placed inside the space like loose objects, contributing to the continuity and cleanliness of the forms.

Ocean House

Cox Richardson

Situated on the upper part of a hill and surrounded by a native forest of aromatic species, this house is hidden in the middle of a natural reserve. It also enjoys spectacular views of the sea in Palm Beach, Australia. The construction is difficult to see from the coast because it blends into the landscape. The volume's warm wood façades look like a sandstorm, while the curved roof appears like a mirage.

The architect Philip Cox, who is also the owner of this weekend home, defined the project as an integration with the landscape. According to Cox, the challenge was to take advantage of and create a dialogue with each element. The result is an interesting and informal experience as the model of a temporary residence. On one hand, the project reconciles comfort and privacy for a family, and on the other, it has the capacity for up to 100 guests, and contains a place to work.

Due to the conditions of the site, especially the inclination of the terrain and the dense vegetation, the volume is planted vertically in three levels that "hang" from the upper part of the mountain. The entrance is created out of the roof, which is connected to the ground through a light extension in the form of a platform. The curved section of the roof creates a small atrium that visually dominates most of the house's living areas. The social zone occupies the intermediate level, and the bedrooms are situated in the lowest part of the composition.

Architect: Cox Richardson
Location: Palm Beach, Australia
Area: 4,516 sq. feet
Photographs: Patrick Bingham–Hall

The construction is partially supported by the face of a cliff. The building gives the impression of pulling away from the cliff, and the spaces are organized lineally in order to give each one an impressive view.

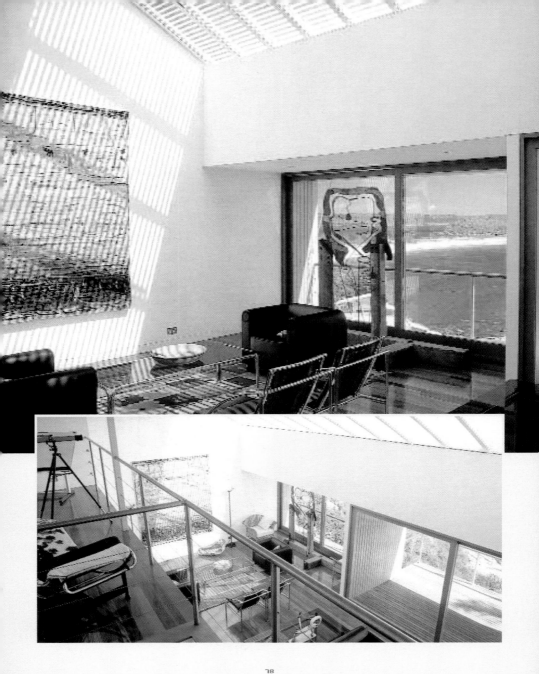

Though the house occupies a large construction area, it is terraced along the slope of the land, affecting the landscape as little as possible. The residence enjoys a view of the sea from the high part of the rocky outcrop.

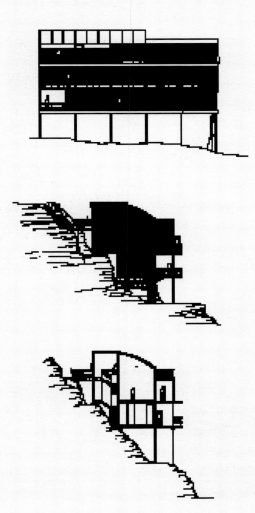

Sections

1. Acces - 2. Living room - 3. Diving room
4. Terrace - 5. Kitchen - 6. Bedroom
7. Bedrooms

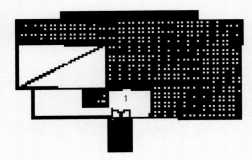

Second floor

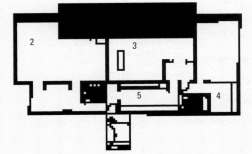

First floor

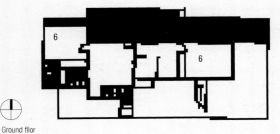

Ground flilor

The openings in the roof provide the interior with various sources of zenithal light. The openings, as well as the translucent canopy that covers part of the main terrace, bathe the house with natural light throughout the day and create a fresh and warm ambience in the interior.

Summer Cabin

Jarmund / Vigsnaes AS Architects MNAL

This small summer house is located on the southern coast of Norway. The cabin is situated in the middle of a forest of oak trees, only a few yards from the beach. The architectural solution aimed to emphasize the boundary between these different natural spaces and to establish an element that reinforces their relationship.

The building is set into the landscape like a wall that divides –yet relates– the beach and the forest. Due to the house's configuration, the forest takes on the character of a private garden. A linear design is organized along a volume with narrow proportions. A double opening in the two façades, at the height of the dining room, connects the two natural environments. The volume's distribution follows the path of the sun: the bedrooms are located in the eastern part, while the living room and the terrace are located in the extreme west.

The project's materials accentuate its light character and consolidate its relationship with the immediate surroundings. A softly inclined plane of oiled oak panels covers the house and reinforces the sensation of lightness. The roof's exposed zinc laminates that again emphasize the construction's light and economical character. The three steps that separate the zones of the dining room and kitchen differentiate the areas and solve the slight inclination of the terrain. The false ceiling continues the double inclination and wood of the roof. Light-colored tiles cover the floors, creating a durable, low-maintenance surface.

Architect: Jarmund / Vigsnaes AS Architects MNAL
Collaborators: Einar Jarmund, Hakon Vigsnaes.
Alessandra Losberg
Location: Norway south coast
Area: 1,290 sq. feet
Construction date: 2000
Photographs: Nils Petter Dale

The design details, including light materials and simple elements like wooden panels, a zinc roof and sliding doors, establish a sober and elegant atmosphere.

The elongated house is situated on the east-west axis in order to make the most of the sun, the distant views of the bay , the ocean towards the north. The entrance, a glass door finished in wood, breaks the continuous façade and frames the visual.

1. Entrance/dining room - 2. Kitchen
3. Living room - 4. Terrace - 5. Bedrooms
6. Main room

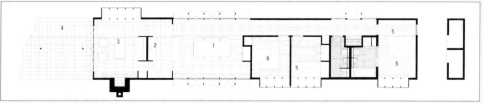

Plan

The materials used for the project, including zinc, wooden strips, and metallic veneer respond to the simplicity of the interior design. The openings to the exterior are like small volumes that intercept the inclined wooden plane, a gesture that gives the project a special plasticity.

The use of light-colored wood in the interior gives the space a certain freshness. The design and decorative elements, like the lamp in the dining room, the chimney and the kitchen cabinets, are specially designed to complement the architecture.

The property in Baja California has magnificent views on its narrow sides, of the sea towards the west and of the mountains towards the east. On its longer sides, the lot is limited by party walls with neighboring plots. The elevation of the land —on a plain 26 feet above the beach— creates a natural balcony above the Pacific Ocean. Located more than 12,5 miles away from the closest village, the land is part of a development. The only service available is water brought down from the mountains. A system of photovoltaic solar panels provides electricity.

A sequence of landscaped spaces located at the back of the plot welcome the visitor. Though the sequence covers the entire property and features limited views of the sea, it is only revealed once inside the house, where openings frame and isolate scenes from the dramatic context.

The composition is based on two main volumes that interrupt the lot's elongated dimensions and create a central space in the middle of both. This central area reinterprets the typology of the Mexican patio. The structures are finished with a fine mortar in a light yellow tone that blends with the color palette of the surrounding desert landscape. A series of walls recovered in local Venetian blue and red tiles intersect and interact with the small buildings to create diverse visual relationships. A third volume contains the master bedroom and is elevated above the rest of the house in order to provide the best views of the ocean and the mountains.

Architect: Leddy Maytum Stacy Architects (before TLMS)
Collaborators: Marsha Maytum, Roberto Sheinberg, Michelle Huber
Location: Rancho Nuevo, Baja California South, Mexico
Area: 4.300 sq.feet
construction date: 2000
Photographs: Undine Pröhl

This sunny getaway, envisioned by its original Alaska-based owners, was inspired by the conditions of the landscape and the isolation of the property.

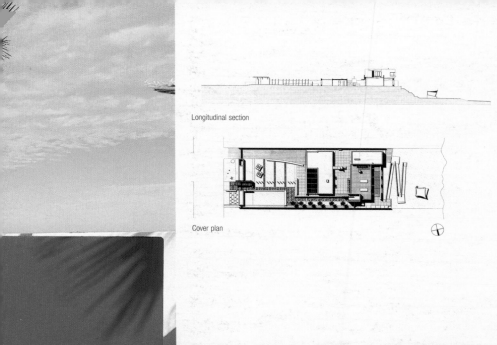

Longitudinal section

Cover plan

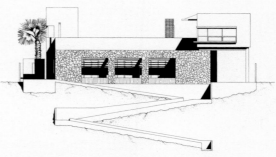

Elevation

Located in the middle of a typical Mexican desert landscape, this simple building pays tribute to the region's vernacular architecture. After crossing the entrance, a long path, formed by walls and a succession of gardens and small plazas, leads the visitor to the house's central space.

1. Entrance - 2. Garden - 3. Orchard - 4. Hall
5. Living room - 6. Dining room - 7. Kitchen
8. Terrace - 9. Bedrooms - 10. Parking
11. Main room

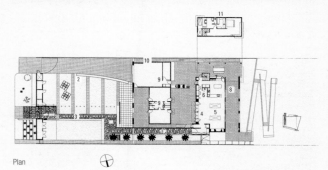

Plan

The structural elements, like the columns and
beams, and the architectural gestures, like the
stairways, walls and windows, form part of the
project's composition. Most of the furnishings are
built into the architecture and express the same
formal language.

Koehler Residence

Julie Snow Architects

The Bay of Fundy is one of the most spectacular —and turbulent— landscapes on the east coast of Canada. The bay is subject to the highest tides in the world, reaching up to 62 feet--equivalent to a five-story building. Also the site of 82-foot waves, the coastline of New Brunswick is the location of this family refuge. The landscape is a reef of granite stone, dotted with pine trees and scarcely populated —making it the ideal location for a private haven with an impressive view of the sea.

The project's design attempted to make the most of the surrounding conditions by placing the building only a few yards from the line of the high sea. The building is elevated to the level of the rocks which support it.

This home's design makes reference to the modern movement, minimalist architecture, and specifically to the Farnsworth House by Mies van der Rohe. The architect Julie Snow created a volume made of two equal bodies, one above the other. In the extreme east of the composition, where the land slopes in a more pronounced manner, the architect created a daring projection on both levels. The structure is supported by slim wooden columns. The north façade features a stone element that gives the composition stability and contains a chimney and storage areas.

The interior is a tranquil, open and continuous space. Upon entering the house from the north façade, an empty space relates the two floors. Continuous windows along the southern façade link the sleeping areas with the living area.

Architect: Julie Snow Architects
Collaborators: Campbell Comeau, John Johnson (engineers) Jack Snow (mechanic) Ed Young (builder)
Location: New Brunswick, Canada
Area: 1,505 sq. feet
Construction date: 2000
Photographs: Brian Vanden Brink

This design of this house creates the sensation of being in front of the ocean, yet it avoids any literal references to a nautical motif.

Bay of Fundy

This house conforms to the terrain through a simple structure, composed of two rectangular elements . The pillars that form the structure extend from the lower part of the pieces and anchor the building to this rugged and rocky plot of land.

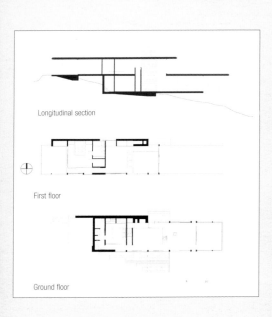

Longitudinal section

First floor

Ground floor

1. Entrance - 2. Living room - 3. Kichen
4. Dining room - 5. Terrace - 6. Bedrooms
7. Living room

The reference to nautical constructions is achieved through the reproduction of spaces and the relationship between the interior and the exterior instead of formal gestures, which would have made a caricature out of the house. The surroundings are more like a dominant and inaccessible landscape –like the ocean from a boat– rather than a utilitarian garden.

The clean lines and the prevalence of wood in the interior space generate a warm and tranquil atmosphere. The spaces are linked with each other and with the exterior view through mobile elements like sliding doors.

Merimbula house

Clinton Murray Architects Pty. Ltd.

This house is constructed almost completely out of restored wood that was recycled from buildings constructed in the '40s. Because of wood's resistant character, the architect used it for the project's entire structural system. However, the floor supports and the window frames came from the demolition of old warehouses. The floors and complete pieces, such as doors, were recycled from an old wool factory.

The house's surroundings are typical of this part of the Australian east coast —a rough and hard environment. The house is organized according to a simple U-shaped scheme that wraps around a patio and captures the morning sunlight. A 41-foot long swimming pool is protected from the neighbors by a fence constructed out of wooden strips. Generally used for the construction of oyster boxes, the strips pay tribute to the local culture, since oyster cultivation is the main industry of Merimbula. A large wooden terrace runs along the entire length of the building, on the side that looks towards the sea and receives the afternoon sun.

The climate in this part of Australia encourages residents to spend more time outdoors than indoors. As a result of this lifestyle and to strengthen the house's relationship with its surroundings, each room has ocean views and its own exterior space. Three guest bedrooms on the main floor are organized like a suite. The upper floor contains the master bedroom, a small living room, a dressing room, a bathroom and a large terrace.

Architect: Clinton Murray
Collaborators: Maxwell Murray
(project director), Andrew Murray (special finishes), Brian, Steven and Trevor Jory (carpentry)
Location: Merimbula, Australia
Area: 3.381 square feet
Construction date: 1997
Photographs: Janusz Molinski

Wood plays the starring role in this house. Recycled wooden pieces with different origins make reference to various cultural elements of this Australian region.

The interior patio, the element that organizes and articulates all the spaces of the house, is an area of great sobriety and formal expressiveness. The openings towards this space are much more controlled than the large, continuous windows that open towards the exterior on the back façade.

1. Entrance - 2. Bedrooms - 3. Kitchen
4. Living room/dining room - 5. Courtyard
6. Swimming pool - 7. Terraces
8. Main bedroom

Ground floor

First plan

North elevation

South elevation

The different origin of the wood pieces created sections and discontinuous elements among the different details. The sum of these variables in the same architectural language is a homogenous and harmonic construction.

Wood plays an important role in the interior. However, the floors are polished and varnished and the vertical partitions and the ceilings are plastered and painted white, creating a counterpoint to the materials on the exterior of the house.

Coromandel House

Fearon Hay Architects

This lot in New Zealand is stretched over the north-south axis and includes two zones with very different landscapes and views. The south part is occupied by a dense forest of lumber pines, while the north side of the property enjoys more distant views across Mercury Bay towards the Great Barrier and Mercury Islands. The land is relatively flat and has narrow and elongated proportions.

Built as a family summer residence, the house's design was quite simple. The main were to provide protection due to its seafront location and to make the most of the setting by promoting the relationship between interior and exterior.

The architectural strategy presented two buildings placed along the site. One is simple with square proportions and set amidst the forest; it contains a guest bedroom, a storage area and a play area. The principal volume, closer to the northern part of the lot, enjoys ocean views and contains the living spaces and the bedrooms. Every room in the house feels the presence of the sea or the surrounding forest.

Thanks to this strategy, the interior spaces can transform from a closed space to a gallery open to the exterior. Large sliding glass doors can be folded to fully integrate the living room, the dining room and the kitchen with the landscape. The terraces on the east and west sides provide access to the beach and the pine forest. The building's alignment gives the upper floor, which contains the master bedroom, a special view of the bay and the islands.

Architect: **Fearon Hay Architects**
Collabortors: **Nil**
Location: **Coromandel Peninsula, New Zealand**
Area: **2.688 sq. feet**
Construction date: **1999**
Photographs: **Patrick Reynolds**

The spaces of this residence and the project's
objectives could best be defined by the word
flexibility. The inhabitants of this summer home
can enjoy various activities in close relationship
with the surroundings.

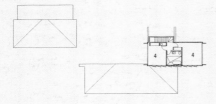

First floor

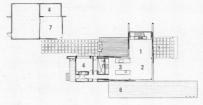

Ground floor

1. Living room - 2. Dining room - 3. Kitchen
4. Bedrooms - 5. Covered terrace - 6. Terrace
7. Playroom

The house features a volumetric play between lively elements that contrast with other solid, heavy elements. The exterior chimney and the stairway are made of stone, while other elements in the house are made of wood, metal or glass.

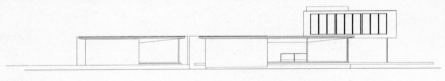

East elevation

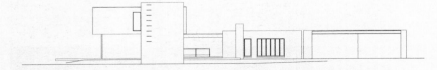

Western elevation

The flexibility of the space is expressed by elements like the sliding doors, the folding windows or the curtains that can divide the spaces in different ways. Proximity to the exterior is ever-present in this project.

Böhler ○ Jutz House

Baumschlager ○ Eberle

Böhler-Jutz House is set on a hill, resting in a landscape, positioned on a sloping site. It is built on three levels, its rooms distributed according to the degree of privacy desired, and they are accessed separately.

The building is of brick, with windows and doors elegantly framed in metal. Handsomely, the window panes reflect the surrounding environment, even from afar. On the highest part of the site is a shallow wading pool that marks a boundary with the difference in grade, which drops from one of the long sides of the pool. This same element serves as a lookout point, protected by a glass guardrail that is almost imperceptible.

At the other end of the house, a containing wall on the site curves into a path that leads to the main door of the house. The stepped layout of the house is the natural result of the hillside terracing used as a practical building measure.

The architectural volume is configured like a closed tower of brick of rather compact appearance which, at the same time, is clearly broken by apertures of different but clearly defined dimensions.

The distribution of the rooms has left the more private areas on the ground floor. The higher level in-cludes a landscaped exterior with terrace and pool, and it is also this level that houses the kitchen, dining room, and living room. The bedrooms are on the lower level. Thus, there are two bedrooms on the mezzanine floor, and four more on the ground floor. The ground floor also houses the study spaces or library.

Architect: Baumschlager ○ Eberle
Location: Dornbirn, Austria
Construction date: 2000
Photographs: Eduard Hueber

The formal composition of the building is rather
serene and it rests comfortably on its site.

The stepped architecture is the result of the hill slope. The particular hierarchy of the levels establishes common areas at the top of the building and areas dedicated to nighttime activities on the lower floors (including the bedrooms).

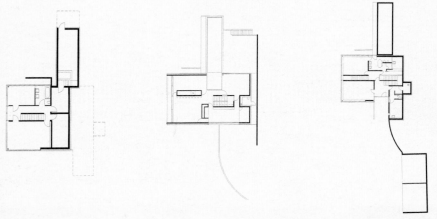

Ground plan   Top floor   Mezzanine

A Naked House

Shigeru Ban Architects

The client for this project stated the precise requisites of the architectural design: a budget of 25,000,000 Yen and the family relationship of those who would live in the building, —the client's mother, himself, his wife, their two kids, and a dog. What he wanted was described as a house providing "enough privacy to be sure the people in the family are not isolated, a house that gives everybody freedom to have individual activities in a shared environment."

The building is close to a river and surrounded by fields with greenhouses. The exterior walls are two panels made of plastic and reinforced fibers, and the nylon fiber inner walls are on a wooden frame. Between both are polyethylene-filled plastic bags that serve as insulation. Through these bags, a pleasant diffuse light penetrates the interior of the house.

The house is a single large space of two stories, with four individual rooms equipped with wheels that can be freely moved. These rooms are small and contain a minimum number of objects, and can also be moved according to the needs of their use. The versatility of these elements makes it possible to place them together and thus create a larger room, eliminating the sliding doors. They can be taken onto the terrace to take full advantage of the interior space or used as an additional flooring for the children's playroom. The result is the architect's vision of an agreeable and flexible way of living which evolved out of the client's idea of promoting family life.

Architect: Shigeru Ban Architects
Location: Kawagoe-shi, Saitama-ken, Japan
Construction date: November 2000
Photographs: Hiroyuki Hirai

Some time for meditation is always necessary before accepting the project for a private residence.

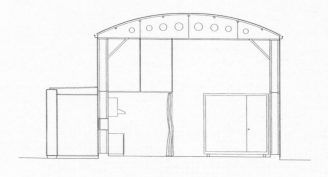

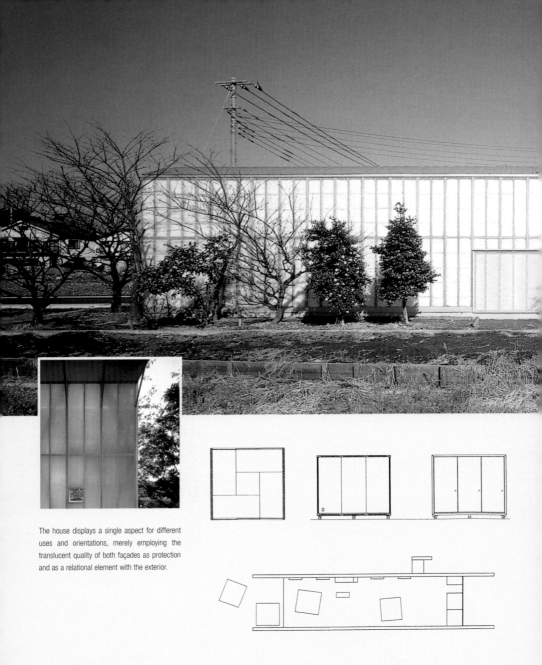

The house displays a single aspect for different uses and orientations, merely employing the translucent quality of both façades as protection and as a relational element with the exterior.

Floor plan distribution of the different stories according to varying decorating proposals for the private-use containers. This mobility can vary at different times of the day, providing the residents with the option of arranging the interior surface area according to the needs of the moment.

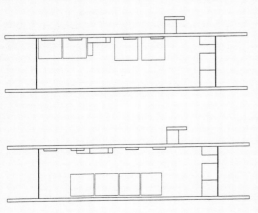

The different containers constitute the desired number of sleeping rooms. The mobility of the pieces allows the dwelling to be used without affecting the "enclosed privacy" of each room.

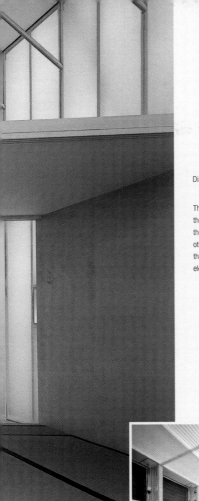

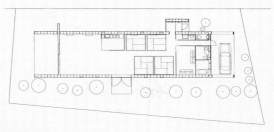

Distribution pattern

The installations and equipment are concealed in the walls of the house. This basic plan explains the thickness of the two main façades, since the other faces can be considered more like windows that frame the views of the exterior, the only fixed element of this project.

The Water Tower

Jo Crepain Architect NV

Based on landscape architect Jan Moereels's commission, the project consisted of remodeling and shoring up a concrete cylindrical water tank. The 13-foot-high cylinder rests on four columns, which rise 75 feet above the ground. Between the columns, 13-foot-square platforms have been inserted, connected by metal stairs. The house in its final version, covered with a native variety of ivy, was to merge with the natural setting.

Moereels's intention was to offer a new vision of the water tower by transforming it into an efficiency apartment, incorporating the inescapable extant platforms. This would be achieved by conserving and emphasizing the structure's original function as an important element in the local environment, using a minimal number of simple building materials.

The columns were completely revealed inside, and the ground floor kitchen and dining room were arranged to open onto the street. A double-height ceiling at the back was fitted with an oversize window to take in the magnificent view of the arroyo and the woodland. The wall of the bedroom is a galvanized screen that can be moved to allow open-air sleeping.

Different metallic stairways connect the separate levels (8 platforms) with the ground. The three sides of the structure that are visible from the street are covered with Reglit glass, while the southern façade uses transparent double-glazed glass. An opening was made in the bottom of the water tank, which is now used for parties and other special occasions.

Architect: **Jo Crepain Architect NV**
Location: **Brasschaat, Belgium**
Construction date: **1997**
Photographs: **Sven Everaert**

The project consisted of remodeling and shoring up a concrete construction used as a cylindrical water tower.

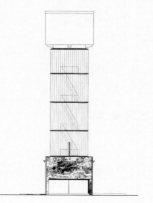

The sheet-metal stairway between levels is of minimal dimensions and is very light, along the lines of stairs used infrequently or for specific purposes.

The refurbishing of this structure, and its surprising change in function, make it a textbook example of a "minimal vertical living space."

The austerity of the materials used and the exposed superstructure of the building give an innovative look to the construction's new domestic functions.

Site plan

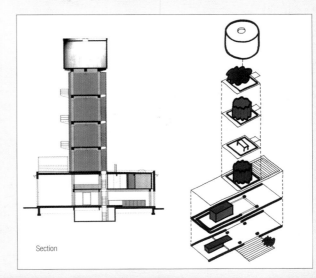

Section

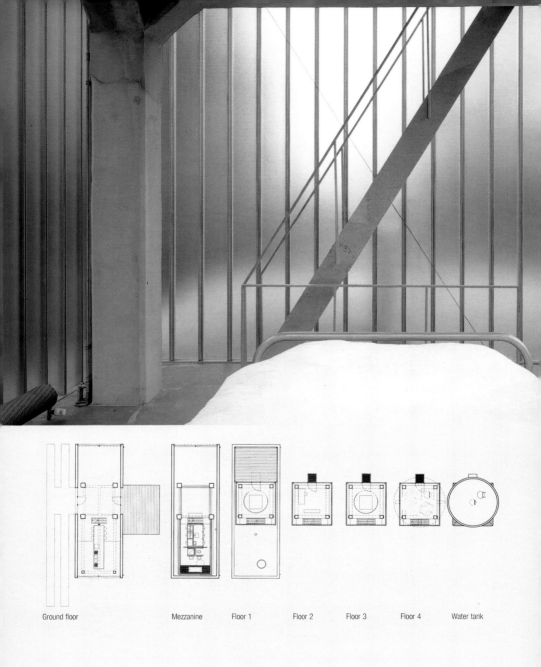

Ground floor   Mezzanine   Floor 1   Floor 2   Floor 3   Floor 4   Water tank

The main room is on the first floor of the cylindrical body, immediately above the living room. This first platform roofs the extension to double-height of the ground floor (where the main and common rooms are--kitchen, dining room, living room, guest room).The rest of the bedrooms are distributed among the other levels. The master bedroom is on the first floor; a second bedroom is on the third floor. Privacy is maintained thanks to sets of circular rails screwed into the ceiling: they serve the curtains circling the bed like old-style canopies.A view of the inside of the tower with different levels serving different functions.

Red house

Fulvio Moruzzi

The strong visual impact of this building on the rocky terrain of the Vallpineda Hill in Sitges, Spain, is due to its attractive and unique forms, brought about by the circular elements that contribute to the massive colorist whole. More than 239 square yards (2,152 square feet) of living space are managed by an aerial platform that uses the terrain to maximum effect.

Three circular structures are attached at a single point of support. A single central column is topped by a white concrete cup-shaped capital. Together, the three structures make up the main frame of the house. The building's verticality is based on a metallic structure of glassed fenestration with red piers. The chimney is painted a gold color and becomes a stabilizing link in the composition.

On the street-leve façade opposite these circular bodies is the main entrance. Beside the front door, still another semicircular element that serves as a canopy juts out from a rounded glass-walled module, like a large mullioned bay window. The back of the site, on the sea side, offsets the main façade by the presence of an imposing pool.

The interiors employ warm colors —red, lime, and gold. The contemporary designer furniture maintains the same novel spirit as the exterior, visible from practically every vantage point thanks to the large windows. A spiral metal staircase originates on the ground floor, leading to the two upper levels and to a walkway that crosses the space to join the rooms on the opposite side.

Architect: Fulvio Moruzzi
Location: Sitges. Barcelona. Spain
Construction date: 1992
Photographs: Stella Rotger

Totally integrated into the natural environment of its location, the construction boldly stands between sea and mountain.

The organic form of the gigantic concrete columns combines with the glass façades that follow the curvature of the plan. The metallic staircase is extended in a walkway crossing the wide space, the only connection between the two ends of the building. All the metallic frames are in red, unifying the materials.

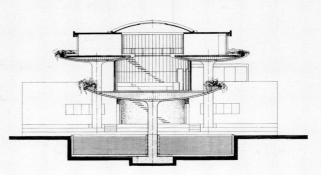

In cross section, the house is defined by its symmetry, which passes un noticed in the finished piece because of the dominant presence of the concrete structure. The cup-shaped capital of the central column serves as protective covering for the pool in the garden.

The circular geometry of the plan creates interior spaces that continue up the full height of the building. The top floor is reminiscent of a balcony that opens to the atrium, configured by the spiral staircase.

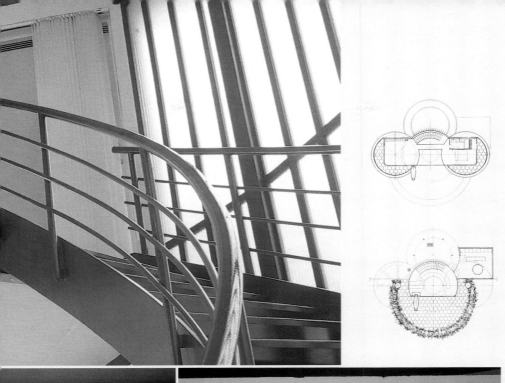

This house, a second residence for a businessman, became a verbal experiment between the architects for the first six months' work, without plans or maquettes. The project is in Santa Ana, San José, Costa Rica. More concretely, it is in the residential zone of Rio de Oro, an area dotted with small, modest houses. Achio House was a quest for all the previous requisites in the program and for integration into the landscape itself.

A translucent linear barrier defines the garage and protects the southern boundaries. An outer wall protects the site itself and establishes the geometry of a terrain whose northern part situates the house obliquely. This permits an integration of the dwelling into the environment and relates interior/exterior without compromising the basic premises of protection and privacy. Large mobile panels aid in achieving this aim, and clearly define the entrance zone and dilute the solidity of the plan's distribution.

A skylight filters natural light into the main entrance. The construction is framed on the basis of an interplay of color volumes: red extends the north/south entrance, where the studio is located, and creates privacy without isolation. A walkway connects this mass with the garage.

The house has three gardens: one inside, one outside next to the pool, and what the architects call a "green garden." The roof of the first story is used as a terrace and also serves as spatial referent.

Architect: Guillermo Garita, Athanasios Haritos
Location: Santa Ana, San José, Costa Rica
Construction Date: 1999
Photographs: Oldemar Rivera Quesada, Guillermo Garita (panoramics views), Athanasios Haritos

The building was structured around an interplay between color volumes.

Large mobile panels aid in the exterior/interior integration.

First floor plan

Ground plan

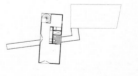

Studio floor plan

The first six months' work were used to define the functional arrangement of the house. From that point on, the first proposals were started.

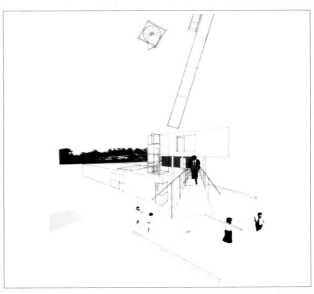

A walkway connects the structure with the garden and the garage area. A skylight centered on the roof of the ground floor lets natural light into the main entrance.

Photographic montage of the last phase of the
construction during which the facings of the pool
were applied.

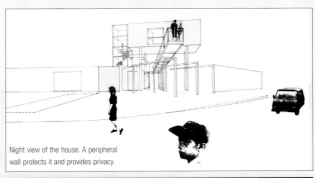

Night view of the house. A peripheral wall protects it and provides privacy.

Flatz House

Baumschlager ◦ Eberle

Flatz House is on the gentle west side of one end of the Schaan neighborhood in the Principality of Liechtenstein. It is destined to be the residence of a doctor and his family, made up of seven children.

Immersed in a landscape of houses built in a traditional rural style, Flatz rises up uniquely with a different look. It has the heaviness of piled up building blocks.

The north façade of the house is completely closed, contributing to the compact look of something like a minimalist sculpture. Its hillside siting makes the building unrevealing of what this four-story residence holds. The basement, for example, houses both wine cellar and garage.

The privileged placement of the site was a decisive factor when establishing the criteria of orientating the functional layout of the dwelling. From the highest levels, the eye can look out and see from the Rhine valley to the outline of the Swiss mountains. The living rooms have big windows that set the tone of the paradisal environment. The closure system includes a double glazing that conserves and controls direct sunlight and the possible thermal contrasts that come about in such extreme climates.

The special qualities of the rooms improve with the direct connection with the outdoors. Hence, we see a terrace with a water tank in one corner of the ground floor. On the first floor, the external space is roofed by the façade of the master bedroom. The second floor is designed for use as the children's spaces.

Architect: **Baumschlager ◦ Eberle**
Location: **Schaan. Liechtenstein**
Construction Date: **2000**
Photographs: **Eduard Hueber**

Inside a landscape of houses built in a traditional rural style, Flatz House rises up uniquely with a different modern look.

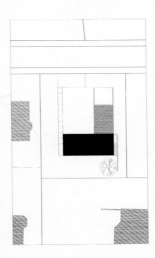

Cross section

The compact aspect of the house is reproduced in each of the elevations in the drawing.

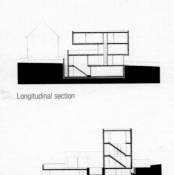

Longitudinal section

Longitudinal section

Four materials stand out in the construction of the house, elevating the functional features and at the same time the elegance of the architecture. The exterior facings of pigmented cement (corn-colored), the interior finishing (white plastic paint), the plane tree wood features, and the green stone.

The living room opens out to a gardened terrace that roofs the lower story.

Allgaier◦gaugg House

Baumschlager ◦ Eberle

The building style of All-gaier-Gaugg is habitual in Lochau. Stairways go up the mountains, offering a boundless horizon. The layout of the sites is narrow, and this, along with the marked incline, makes for buildings that resemble watchtowers along the mountains.

Allgaier-Gaugg's two main structures define it through the plain, contrasting materials used. One of the salient parts unifies all the different functions of the house, from the way it is entered by the upper-level catwalk to the lowest subgrade features. The building's two highest levels are used as living quarters; the lower levels become an individual apartment and a subgrade office.

The priorities defining the different uses of the building are reflected in the differentiating concept in the closure system. While the apartment and the office are accessed from the side, a catwalk on the southern façade beside the garage is used to enter the family unit. The distinctive layout of both areas lies in the different materials used. The building with masonry walls has a cavity wall (ventilated brick); the catwalk is a metal structure below the glassed passageway leading to the main body of the building.

Architect: **Baumschlager ◦ Eberle**
Location: **Lochau. Austria**
Construction Date: **1998**
Photographs: **Eduard Hueber**

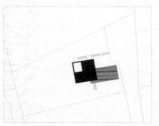

The building style of Allgaier-Gaugg is traditional in Lochau. Stairways go up the mountains, offering a boundless horizon.

South elevation

North elevation

West elevation

East elevation

The three floors used as living quarters are distinguished by the direct ventilation systems in the kitchens and bathrooms. Both the individual and the family apartments are connected by an interior stairway.

Cross section

Fourth floor

Third floor

Second floor

Ground floor

440 House

Fougeron Architecture

This house in Palo Alto, California, is a 4,483-square-foot duplex designed by a couple. The house, glassed in and on a free plan, incorporates the latest technologies applicable to building. These technologies include new glass products from England and cutting-edge framing systems. The exposed steel superstructure (beams, joists, air-conditioning) make it clear that this complex system meets the California seismic codes (it includes seismic damping assemblies). Natural light from different directions (floors, ceilings, walls) is combined with translucent, transparent, and reflecting materials to create visually dynamic spaces.

The house is organized around the central axis, taking in the living room and flanked by the glassed volume and a room used for storage and services. This space was originally conceived as a transparent link between the garden area in back and the front lawn.

The channel formed by the double-height zone, with glass walls and sand-blasted glass floors, delineates the building. The transparency is again reinforced by the inhabitants' direct contact with the landscape architecture. A bridge crossing the living room connects the rooms on the opposite side.

The whole project was conceived as a conflation of materials, walls, floors, and furniture. The idea was to create a simple stage which, in spite of reductions, would be full of visual surprises and suggestive planes. The result is a way of drawing and building a dwelling type for the coming years.

Architect: **Fougeron Architecture**
Location: **Palo Alto, California, U.S.A.**
Construction date: **1999**
Photographs: **Richard Barnes**

This residence is a clear example of contemporary aesthetics. The house, glassed in and on a free plan, incorporates the latest technologies applicable to building.

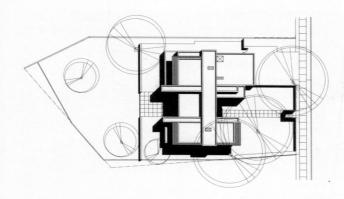

The open plan creates a visual continuity between the living room and the rest of the rooms in the house. The use of translucent materials in the walls contributes to this effect.

Both the longitudinal and the cross sections of the building reflect the spatial continuity that predominates in the design.

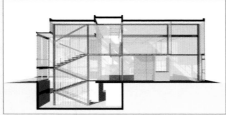

Perspective section through the family area

Perspective section through the stairwell

The main staircase, which is made of metal, has its own glassed-in volume. This creates one of the main focuses of the house. The vertical axis here becomes a channel for both natural and artificial light.

Plan of first floor

Plan of second floor

Howard House

Bryan MacKay-Lyons

This project near the coast of Nova Scotia resembles a huge wall housing domestic activities. The façades of this enormous building are covered with corrugated aluminum, galvanized to protect the metal from the rain and sea salt. In contrast to the bucolic surroundings, it has an industrial look, yet it is reminiscent of the austere buildings typical of the area.

The reinforced concrete foundations emerge from the ground to form a socle that bears witness to the difficulty of erecting a building in a place where the water level is constantly variable. In addition to this solid concrete plinth, there is a concrete staircase, attached to the main structure, which provides shelter from the icy west winds and thermal isolation for the house. The roof, which slopes in one direction, rises toward the south, covering one continuous space that contains a garage, entrance patio, kitchen, living room, and projecting balcony. Some elements, such as the fireplace, the interior bridge, and the glass-covered southern façade, create interesting shapes and angles, adding small, comfortable areas that enrich the home.

The structural skeleton can be seen throughout the house: the metal truss dominates the loft and the wooden frame is exposed in various segments of the ceiling and walls. The overall result is a practical, sculptural, minimalist work, influenced by the austerity of the local architecture and blending with the setting.

Architect: Bryan MacKay-Lyons
Collaborators: Niall Savage and Trevor Davies
Construction date: 1999
Location: West Pennant, Nova Scotia, Canada
Area: 1950 sq. feet
Photographs: Undine Pröhl

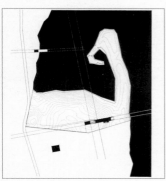

From the outside, the house designed by Bryan MacKay-Lyons looks almost impenetrable due to the homogeneity of the galvanized corrugated aluminum facade. The interior is done in warm materials, such as wood and ceramic. The huge windows help bring the outside in.

The kitchen floor is polished and waxed cement. The same material covers the lower parts of the concrete facade, affording continuity to the different levels.

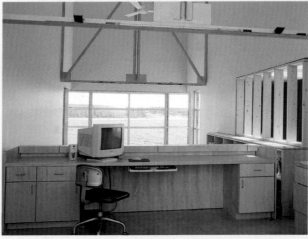

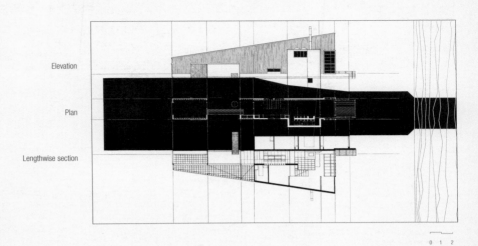

Elevation

Plan

Lengthwise section

0 1 2

Marmonier Villa

Rudy Ricciotti

This project by Rudy Ricciotti consisted of remodeling and expanding a 1930's villa. He wanted to open the house up to the adjacent forest and enhance the views of the distant Mediterranean.

The lush plant life that surrounds the house and the moderate climate gave him a perfect opportunity to build a terrace with swimming pool. The pronounced slope of the land made it necessary to place both elements on a surface that projects above the landscape. To avoid having to use railings that would mar the views of the countryside, the swimming pool was placed on the edge of the platform. A net was installed below the retaining wall in case of falls.

A 176 sq. feet room leading to the terrace was added to the original building. To emphasize the relationship with the outdoors, the exterior wall is all glass, and there is no trim; the glass panels are joined to each other and to the floor with clear silicone. The roof is a large exposed concrete box that contains earth in which to plant shrubs. This dual function requires certain specific construction details, such as drainage for excess water, which is channeled off through tiny spouts. Supported by the exterior wall, the roof seems to float above the room.

Inside, the floor is wood and the walls are stucco. The simplicity of the lines contrasts with the materials of the old house: ceramic tile, painted textured stone, and wooden shutters. The furniture chosen for the new space, designed by the architect, emphasizes these contrasts.

Architect: Rudy Ricciotti
Construction date: 1999
Location: La Garde, France
Area: 2680 sq. feet
Photographs: Philippe Ruault

The swimming pool, 23 m. long and 1.8 m. wide, was placed at the edge of the terrace to avoid having to use railings that would mar the views of the olive grove and cork oaks.

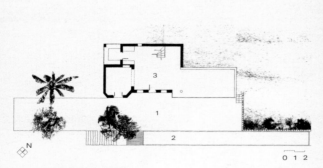

1. Terrace - 2. Swimming pool - 3. Addition

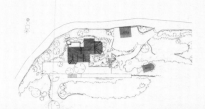

De Blas House

Alberto Campo Baeza

The De Blas house is a brilliant piece of architecture which consists of a glass structure on top of a concrete block sitting on the crest of a hill southeast of Madrid that looks north toward splendid mountains.

The concrete structure is anchored to the ground and appears solid and unyielding. In addition to providing space for the domestic functions, it serves as a vantage point from which to take in the beauty of the landscape. On the northern side, the square windows frame exquisite views, and on the southern side, the light and sky filter through tiny openings in the uppermost part of the wall.

The glass structure, resting atop the platform, is a vantage point accessed from inside the house. The glass walls are become intangible boundaries between interior and exterior. The roof, a sheet of white-painted steel, tops the belvedere. The supporting structure consists of eight double columns with a U-shaped section.

The composition of the materials, thorough attention to architectural detail, suggestive use of light, and variety of sensations it engenders, make the De Blas house both innovative and enduring. The architect who collaborated on this project, Raúl del Valle González, points out the timelessness of Campo Baeza's work: "Beyond the ages, fashions, and styles, beyond time itself, he builds a Greek temple on the eve of the twenty-first century, and transforms the closed, dark, and secret cell of the gods into a transparent, luminous enclosure for man's enjoyment."

Architect: **Alberto Campo Baeza**
Collaborators: **Raúl del Valle González**
and **M.ª Concepción Pérez Gutiérrez**
Construction date: **2000**
Location: **Sevilla la Nueva, Spain**
Area: **2645 sq. feet**
Photographs: **Hisao Suzuki**

At one end of the concrete platform is a small swimming pool which, besides cooling the air in summer, is the source of countless reflections that play over the exterior walls and roof.

Site plan

Alberto Campo Baeza's sketches show the process of determining how to anchor the building on the land: the slope of the ground becomes a refuge on top of which the vantage point is constructed.

N

Second floor

1. Kitchen - 2. Dining room - 3. Living room
4. Bedrooms - 5. Bathrooms - 6. Swimming pool

Western elevation

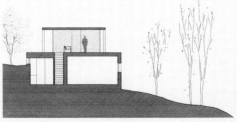

Cross-section

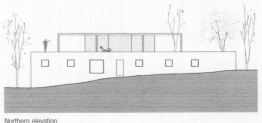

Northern elevation

Ground floor

Unlike the belevedere, the lower level is a solid
unit. The northern façade has large square openings for panoramic views, while the south-facing
exterior wall is dotted by just a few small windows
near the top.

House and Art Gallery

Kennedy ○ Violich Architecture

This project by architects Kennedy and Violich incorporates an art gallery into an existing house. Their task included exterior landscape design to make it possible to exhibit works of art near the adjoining woods. The building had to fulfill varied functions in a single continuous space with abundant wall surfaces for hanging large paintings, works by Warhol, Oldenburg, and Christo, as well as small paintings and engravings. Other requirements included permitting views of the woods and allowing natural light to enter the art gallery while preventing the sun's rays from damaging the artwork.

The designers created a continuous series of six roof levels that join the existing building to the extension, which is organized around a 46- foot long swimming pool. Above it is a skylight that reflects the light from the west and directs it to the exhibit area. At night, this well of light acts like a vacuum where the light from the ceiling bulbs is reflected and creates a serene, constant environment.

The loft in which the study is located has a plywood floor which houses the telecommunications cabling and slopes to become an access ramp and accommodate shelving.

This house redefines the arrangement of household, leisure, and work space, and offers a setting for art which is a clear alternative to institutionalized museums and galleries. The project enriches the typical residential plans with new experiences, and inspires the clients to enjoy their works of art while they work and live.

Architect: Kennedy ○ Violich Architecture
Construction date: 1998
Location: Western Massachussets, USA
Area: 6260 sq. feet
Photographs: Undine Pröhl

The swimming pool starts in the center of the gallery and extends to the ends of the building, to terminate in the projection overlooking the sculpture patio. The socle is reinforced concrete. The sides are covered with stone from the entry level on up.

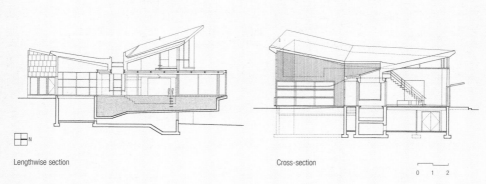

Lengthwise section

Cross-section

0 1 2

The swimming pool is framed by a system of light ironwork that has been painted black. The ceiling of this small area is made of aluminum sheets, which reflect the light from the enormous windows onto the water.

The study floor is part of a plywood surface that starts with the stairs, which go up to the loft and turn to pass above the swimming pool. It also forms shelving with state-of-the-art technology.

Flexible wood surfaces that can be shaped and at
the same time leave hollows for pulling cables
serve as both a structural and finishing element.

1. Swimming pool - 2. Art gallery - 3. Study
4. Pre-existing house

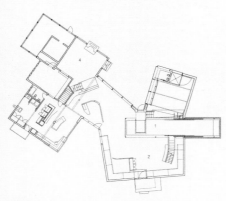

First floor

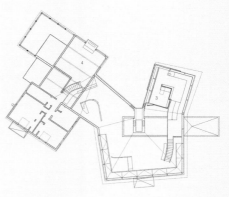

Second floor

Lingg House

Dietrich ○ Untertrifaller Architekten

The Lingg House is located on a hill on the outskirts of the city of Bregenz, with exceptional views of Lake Costanza. To the northeast, the structure is built into the ground to protect it from the coldest temperatures and increase the thermal inertia.

Due to construction complications and the additional expenses for moving earth, the house was set on a perpendicular with the slope. Only the part of the garden that faces south is actually at ground level. The ground floor, which serves as a socle for the house, is concrete and includes the entrance, the garage, and utility rooms. The second floor extends almost two meters out from the entrance, creating a comfortable, quiet intermediate space for greeting guests.

All the bedrooms are on the second floor. The children's rooms have direct access to the garden, and the parents' room enjoys views of the lake, thanks to the huge window in the western façade. To minimize traffic on this level, the stairs are positioned along one of the outer walls; they interfere with no domestic activity. On the third floor, the compartmentalization disappears and the living room, kitchen, and dining room occupy a single space, ending with the exterior balcony, which is covered by an extension of the roof. A narrow corridor connects the balcony with the higher ground. The facades combine different materials: concrete, metal strips, and plywood, chosen for their functional versatility and colors that contrast with the surroundings.

Architect: Dietrich ○ Untertrifaller Architekten
Collaborators: Marina Hämmerle and Albert Rüf
Construction date: 2000
Location: Bregenz, Austria
Area: 4300 sq. feet
Photographs: Ignacio Martinez

At night, the lights accentuate the compositional rhythm of the windows. The higher up you go, the more transparent are the exterior walls.

Architects Dietrich and Untertrifaller gave priority to the placement of the many rooms with respect to the exterior. The strategic placement of the bedrooms and the common area means that all the spaces have large windows. In some places, translucent glass was used for the sake of privacy.

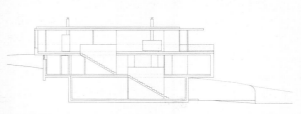

Lengthwise section

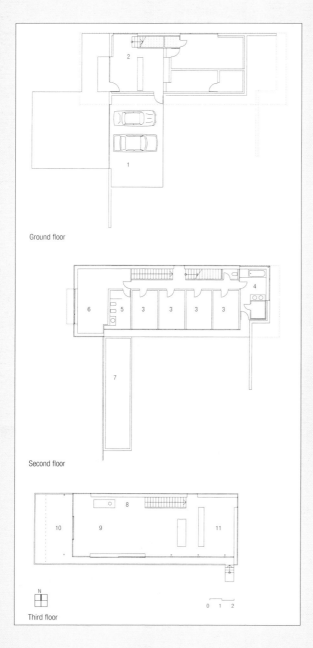

Ground floor

Second floor

Third floor

N

0 1 2

1. Garage - 2. Entrance - 3. Bedrooms
4. Lavatory - 5. Bathroom - 6. Master bedroom
7. Swimming pool - 8. Fireplace - 9. Living room
10. Balcony - 11. Kitchen

McMackin Residence

Price Harrison

This project was to preserve the indigenous countryside and the building was to have a terrace from which the beautiful view could be savored. To emphasize the relationship between the terraced areas and the residence while enhancing the views, the surrounding walls were built very low to the ground.

Platforms connected by small sets of stairs even out the slight irregularities of the terrain. The swimming pool occupies one corner of the grouping and is protected by low walls that ensure privacy without blocking the view. A patio at the entrance divides the house into two sections: one consists of two floors containing the common areas, while the other, just one story high, contains the master bedroom and the garage.

The walls of the various rooms reflect their functions: the foyer, living room, and dining room are almost entirely enclosed by glass, while the more intimate spaces, such as the bedrooms and bathrooms, have just one small, elongated window. The alternating of transparent and opaque walls, and the placement of the openings, result in an aesthetically interesting arrangement which meets the users' needs.

The choice of materials took the setting into consideration, paying tribute to the natural beauty of the area while defining the minimalist architectural shapes of the two sections. The roof and drain holes are brass; the terraces, concrete; and the tops of the walls are limestone. The interior was finished in light wood, plaster and mahogany.

Architect: Price Harrison
Collaborator: Marilyn McMackin
Construction date: 1996
Location: Nashville, Tenessee, USA
Area: 3495 sq. feet
Photographs: Catherine Tighe

Sometimes, the only thing separating the indoors from mother nature is glass. Intermediate spaces, such as terraces, were avoided to give the users a direct view of the surroundings.

The furniture was carefully chosen by the owner, who worked closely with the architect on planning the interiors. The light tones create a warm, bright atmosphere.

The kitchen contains one piece of furniture without wood or stainless steel, facing a row of cupboards. The strategic placement of a window between the two rows of cupboards allows users to enjoy the scenery while washing dishes.

1. Living room - 2. Kitchen - 3. Lavatory
4. Dining room - 5. Entrance - 6. Laundry room
7. Master bedroom - 8. Office - 9. Gym
10. Closets - 11. Bathroom - 12. Garage
13. Fountain - 14. Swimming pool
15. Bedrooms - 16. Study

Ground floor

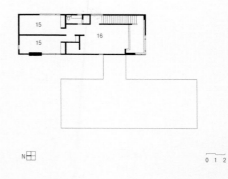

Second floor

N

0 1 2

The small windows in the staircase and private rooms provide continuous illumination. When the sun is in the right place, bright shafts of light shine directly into corners or on objects.

Crescent House

Ken Shuttleworth

The house is set in the heart of Wiltshire, one of the most beautiful rural areas in England. The site is accessed through a gate hidden among the trees. A large curved wall greets the visitor an leads to the entrance with view to a magnificent garden.

All the private spaces are located in the semicircular structure facing northwest, which is opaque to provide protection from the wind and ensure privacy. A semicircle facing southeast has views of the garden, thanks to a glass wall. The dining room, kitchen, and living room are in a single continuous space with 11-foot ceilings, flooded with natural light and in direct contact with the surrounding natural environment. All the traffic areas are concentrated in the intermediate gallery, which provides a transition between the common area and private spaces.

From the outset, the design was influenced by an intense ecological awareness. More than a thousand trees were planted. Those closest to the building protect it from the wind, provide shade in the summer, and let the sunlight pass through in the winter. Thermal insulation was installed in the walls and ceiling, and an area was set aside for solar plates and receptacles for collecting rainwater.

In keeping with local tradition, the house was painted entirely in white. The effect is one of abundant luminosity that changes with the curvature of the walls or the appearance of windows, molding the environment to reflect the time of day and season of the year.

Architect: Ken Shuttlerworth
Collaborators: Ove Arup ∘ Partners (structures)
Construction date: 1998
Location: Wiltshire, United Kingdom
Area: 3225 sq. feet
Photographs: Nigel Young

To the southeast, the Crescent House opens onto a splendid garden. The large glass wall blurs the distinction between indoors and outdoors. At the rear of the house, light filters through high windows, making the private rooms more intimate and peaceful.

1. Entrance - 2. Dining room - 3. Kitchen
4. Dining room - 5. Bedrooms
6. Master bedroom - 7. Living room

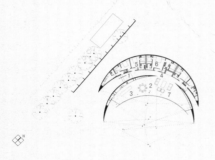

Site plan

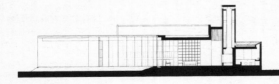

Lengthwise section

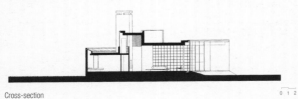

Cross-section

A profound ecological awareness governed the entire design process. No trees were cut down, and more than a thousand were planted to establish an energy-saving microclimate.

An area for solar plates and rainwater storage was provided.

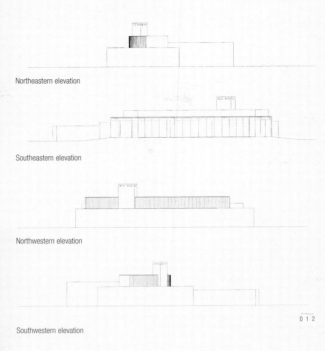

Northeastern elevation

Southeastern elevation

Northwestern elevation

0 1 2

Southwestern elevation

The atmosphere in the domestic areas changes with the seasons. On the one hand, the light leaves the mark of every season, and on the other, the decorative elements, such as cushions and vases, change in contrast with the climate: red for winter, yellow for spring, blue for summer, and green for autumn.

Häfenberg House

Gerold Wiederin

The house sits on a hill with magnificent views of Dornbirn, in the Austrian region of Vorarlberg, known for the quantity and quality of its architectural projects. To take advantage of the views and natural light, Gerold Wiederin placed the new house at the edge of the incline.

The two floors are staggered, creating a balcony on the eastern side. Both the eastern and western facades are glass, while the northern and southern sides are compact and closed except for two small windows. The brick walls are covered with a greenish-gray mineral mixture that emphasizes the project's solidity and produces reflections that play over the house, giving it an iridescence under the sunlight. The lower floor, comprised of open, continuous spaces, is organized around a wooden core that houses the installations and means of access. Large glass doors open onto the terraces, and the polished concrete floor that covers the entire level emphasizes the relationship between both spaces.

The upper level boasts a wide corridor that runs north-to-south and will be converted into a library. Its windows provide a whole new set of views that change the atmosphere of the residence. The flooring, made of small pieces of wood, gives this level a warm, comfortable feeling.

The exterior spaces await the intervention of landscape architects Kienast & Vogt, who will add the finishing touches to the site and shape concise, definitive vistas with their placement of trees and shrubs.

Architect: Gerold Wiederin
Construction date: 1999
Location: Dornbirn, Austria
Area: 2850 sq. feet
Photographer: A.T. Neubau

The Häfenberg house is a fine example of Vorarlberg's flourishing architecture. Gerold Wiederin takes his place alongside such greats as Baumschlager & Eberle or Diertich & Untertrifaller, having participated in the creation of an architectural paradise in this Austrian region.

Austrian architect Gerold Wiederin's work is parallel to the existing building. The intent was to evoke the farm buildings, such as stables and barns, that are common locally.

The warm interior finishes, such as wood and polished concrete, contrast with a cold, heavy exterior.

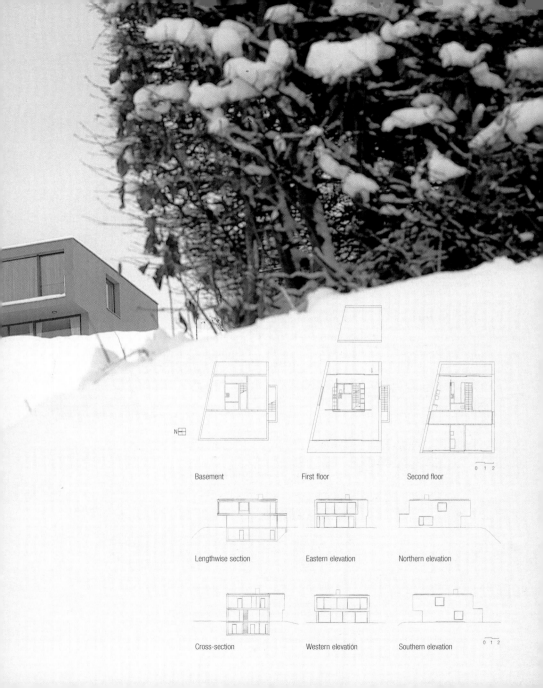

N

Basement	First floor	Second floor

0 1 2

Lengthwise section	Eastern elevation	Northern elevation

Cross-section	Western elevation	Southern elevation

0 1 2

The project by Grupo LBC (Alfonso López Baz and Javier Calleja Ariñol) consists of two elegant buildings resting on a hillock amid the landscaped plain of the San Rafael ranch outside the city of Celaya. Since it is a horse ranch, much of its ten hectares are landscaped and divided into corrals where the horses train and rest.

The residence overlooks the main showjumping ring, which is near an area thick with hundred-year-old trees. From a distance, the complex is made up of white fences dividing the pastures and contrasting with the green hues of the landscaped areas. The plan consists of two structures, simultaneously joined and separated by a mirror of water that has both practical and aesthetic functions. As it produces reflections it increases the humidity and the sensation of coolness in a dry climate where it is not unusual for the temperature to reach forty degrees centigrade. Above the water, wooden footbridges connect the two structures.

The structures are covered by vaulted ceilings. The curvilinear shape of these ceilings allows for uniform reflection of the natural light that enters through the facades. The service rooms and fireplaces were set against the front and back walls, which have hardly any openings to the outside. The lateral walls have huge windows which face the showjumping rings. Around the house are several terraces covered by canvas stretched over poles. These provide shade and views of the plain unhampered by glare.

Architect: Grupo LBC

Collaborators:

Guillermo Flores and Octavio Cardozo

Construction date: 1996

Location: Celaya, Mexico

Area: 3870 sq. feet

Photographs: Fernando Cordero

The vaulted roof is completely smooth, with nothing to detract from enjoyment of its beauty. The lights and ventilation grilles were placed on the walls.

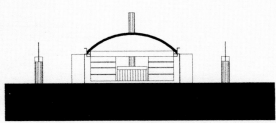

The lengthwise windows in the living room were installed without woodwork so the views would be clear and direct. Access to this room is through a door in one of the corners.

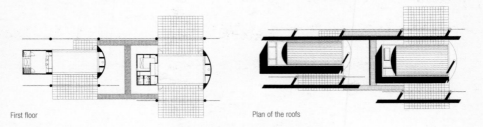

First floor

Plan of the roofs

N

0 1 2

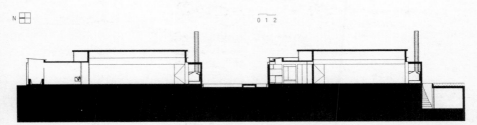

Lengthwise section

Borden-Wiegner Residence

Bart Prince

For years, the clients of the Borden-Wiegner residence had dreamed of leaving the hustle and bustle of Jémez Springs, New Mexico, and building a house in the country. They started by buying a charming lot on the banks of the Jémez River, with views of the tableland and scores of poplars. After living for some time in a trailer on the land, they hired Prince to design their dream house.

Because of the risk of flooding, the house was built on a platform supported by pine posts. Laminated wood beams support the framework. The house is symmetrical on both sides of a central staircase. Each floor has a balcony that almost completely surrounds it.

The lower floor of the residence contains the common areas (kitchen, living room, dining room, and office) and a guest room. The bedrooms are on the middle floor, and the loft boasts a spectacular balcony.

The uniqueness of the materials and construction details employed by Bart Prince complicated the search for a builder.

The outer walls were covered with corrugated metal siding, except, of course, for the window areas. The balcony railings are slender metal slats supported by uprights that provide a sense of continuity. In addition, the galvanized metal and glass staircase rises above the façade. The metal finish reflects the sunlight in myriad ways and gives the house a futuristic appearance.

Architect: Bart Prince
Collaborator: J. Kory Baker
Construction date: 1998
Location: Jémez Springs, New Mexico, USA
Area: 1800 sq. feet
Photographs: Robert Borden, Lewis Wilson and Christopher Mead

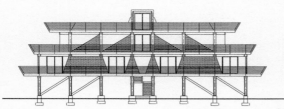

The metal facades give the house a futuristic appearance. The neighbors have dubbed it "the spaceship." It is not surprising that the owners often see curiosity-seekers stopping on the road to marvel at this unique structure. To ensure that the house would blend with the landscape, Bart Prince decided to make it appear light: the posts on which it rests allow the vast expanse of the land to be seen. The spaces between the balconies also keep the views of the natural surroundings from being blocked.

Southern elevation

Northern elevation

The amount of floor space decreases gradually for functional reasons and to take advantage of the sun and the magnificent blue sky. Each level enjoys a generous balcony.

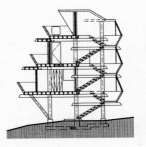 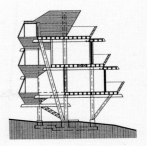

Cross-section   Cross-section

Bart Prince's unique, abstract works are not the result of esthetic whim, but reflect the needs of a society and a place. The Borden-Wiegener house is a real tribute to the mountains and deserts of the New Mexico landscape.

1 Study - 2 Bathroom - 3 Guest room
4 Kitchen - 5 Dining room - 6 Living room
7 Balcony

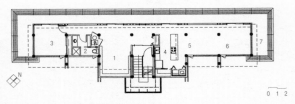

First floor

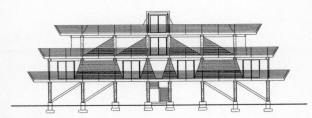

Western elevation

Eastern elevation

Schmitz House

Felipe Assadi Figueroa

This house, designed for a couple, is located between the Andes and the coastal mountains of Chile, and the nearest views are of lush eucalyptus forests to the north and south. The meter-high foliage suggested a new level for the floor so views of the landscape would not be obstructed.

The plan called for a concrete box, a 3 feet high and 8.8 feet wide, facing east-west, that would accommodate the swimming pool and the basement as well as serving as the foundation of the house. Above it is the first floor: a glass and larch structure with the common areas occupying a single, diaphanous space. The upper level, perpendicular to the rest of the grouping, is exposed concrete. Part of this floor projects outward from the building, casting short shadows on the lower facades. The different boxes of which the house is constructed were joined together by a common wall. Attached to this wall is the staircase that leads from the basement to the two upper floors.

The permeability of the structure is in accordance with the amount of privacy required, given the purpose of the different rooms. So, the living room is enclosed entirely in glass, while the master bedroom is mostly opaque.

Thanks to the sunlight, the green glass of the exterior creates colors, transparencies, and reflections which, from the outside, establish a dialogue with the surrounding natural elements. From within, the limits of the space extend to the trees; the space is determined by the immediate surroundings.

Architect: **Felipe Assadi Figueroa**
Collaborators: **Jorge Manieu and Rodrigo Amunátegui**
Construction date: **2001**
Location: **Calera de Tango, Chile**
Area: **3225 sq. feet**
Photographs: **Juan Purcell**

The foundation also serves as retaining walls for the swimming pool. The terrace, which can be used as a diving platform, was covered with dark wooden slats that contrast with the exposed concrete. The flat terrace on the upper level, which is accessed from the bedroom and study, takes up the entire roof.

Computer simulations made it possible to visualize the project before it was built, including the effects of the light and the placement of the furniture. Thus, the client and the architect were able to make changes based on a more realistic idea of what the house would be like.

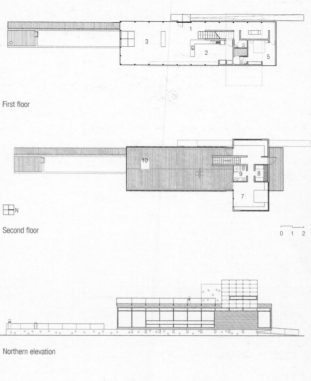

First floor

N

Second floor

0 1 2

Northern elevation

1. Entrance - 2. Kitchen - 3. Living room
4. Swimming pool - 5. Bedroom - 6. Lavatories
7. Bedroom - 8. Dressing room - 9. Bathroom
10. Terrace

Southern elevation

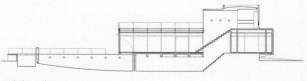

Lengthwise section

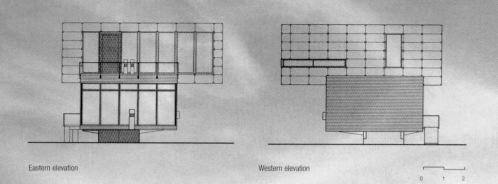

Eastern elevation

Western elevation

0 1 2

The kitchen furnishings consist of two rows of cupboards supported by slender metal poles. Translucent panels between the counter and the upper cupboards help the room blend with the rest of the house. The fact that the cupboards do not extend to the floor or ceiling enhances this effect.

The site of this light construction in New Zealand is a soft hill that ascends towards the coast until it reaches the beach.

The challenge was to create a flexible beach house that would solve the sleeping areas in an independent way and that would provide a basic kitchen/dining room and a living area that could be expanded, if necessary.

The plan started with two independent cabins, each with a loft, that provide a separate space and privacy for the two families when they are there together. If only one family is there, the parents and children can have their own quarters. The two cabins, located in the extremes of the construction, define the central space that is used as a living room and is linked to the exterior.

On the north side, a terrace –a wooden platform– stretches out and is lightly supported by the terrain, ultimately connecting the interior to the hill. On the southern side, where the entrance is located, there is a balcony above ground level that is protected by a wooden pergola covered with canvas for the hottest afternoons. The inclined roof expresses the sloping ground and its opening towards the sea.

The exposed structure and interior coverings are made of wood, a light material that maintains a dialogue with the vernacular constructions of the region. The zinc roof has been recovered inside with wooden panels for better thermal insulation. Sliding windows and latticework cross ventilate in order to maintain a comfortable temperature inside.

Architect: Patrick Clifford Arquitectus Bowes Clifford Thomson
Collaborators: Michael Thomson, Rod Sellas, Tim Mein, Giles Reid
Location: Medlands Beach, Gran Barrier Island, New Zealand
Area: 1,054 sq. feet
Construction date: 1994
Photographs: Patrick Reynolds

Two factors determined the design of this weekend cabin: the special needs of the occupants,
two families, and the structure's proximity to the
sea, even though the view is obstructed by a hill.

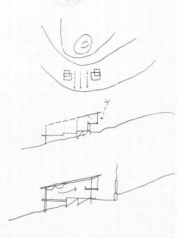

To resolve the slope on which the house is situated, the architect designed an elevated platform, reached by way of a staircase. The platform contains the communal areas of the house and the stairway connects it to the same level in the back part. The space below the platform is used to store water.

1. Living room/Dining room - 2. Kitchen
3. Terrace - 4. Bedrooms

Frontal elevation

Plan

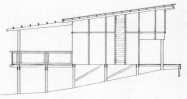

Lateral elevation

Wood is the predominant material in the cabin, in terms of structure and interior finishes, including the terrace and some of the furnishings. Wood emphasizes the light feel of the construction and its integration with the surrounding landscape.

House in Formentera

Bill Wright ○ Nacho Alonso

This residence is located on Formentera, the smallest island of the Balearic archipelago, in Spain. The land is rocky and precipitous and the vegetation is scarce due to the strong winds. On account of the geography, the building had to be placed on the high part of the plain that makes up most of the island. The house's location permitted spectacular views in all directions and turned the house into an object exposed to its surroundings.

The project began by respectfully introducing the building into the natural landscape. The architecture followed the island traditions. The materials, finishes and height of the building make it a discreet object that merges with its setting. The only interruptions are large openings that frame the sea.
The volumetric play allowed the architect to create diverse situations in the interior that meet the requirements for comfortable living. Various terraces stretch out and can be used according to the season, the orientation, or the winds.

The island's traditional construction techniques inspired the materials, details and finishes. The bedroom walls feature an exaggerated inclination and are treated with a rough finish with a white cement base, natural pigments, earth from the local quarry and gray gravel. The other rooms are vertical and have a smooth finish. The bedrooms are treated like isolated elements that organized themselves across the living spaces. The owner designed and created the interior and exterior details and finishes.

Architects: William D. Wright Torrance and Tomas I. Alonso Prieto
Collaborators: Miro Michalec
Location: Punta Prima, Formentera, Spain
Area: 4,054 sq. feet
Date: 2000
Photographs: Pere Planells

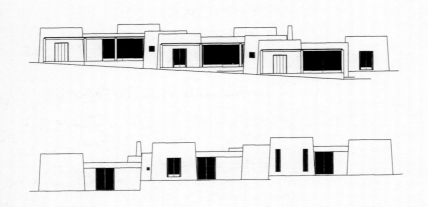

A succession of volumes blend with the surrounding landscape thanks to the techniques, materials and colors used to create the effect of an architecture that emerges from the land.

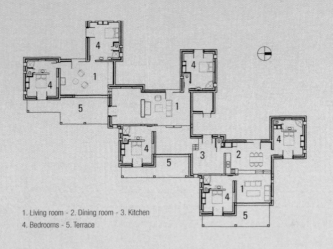

1. Living room - 2. Dining room - 3. Kitchen
4. Bedrooms - 5. Terrace

The volumetric arrangement of the house creates the effect that the interior and exterior spaces integrate with the landscape. The double openings of the spaces enable the side terraces to enjoy the immediate surroundings as well as the view framed by the house towards the west.

The kitchen is an open, flexible space situated in an area that serves as a hinge in the project. The small, star-shaped skylights in the ceiling complement the natural lighting and create a play of light on the floor.

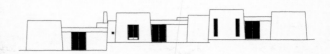

Western elevation

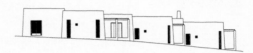

South elevation

Vally Martelli House

Mario Connio

This vacation home is located in Punta Piedras, Uruguay. Dramatic changes in temperature are common, and intense winds constantly whip the coast. The elongated parcel determined the positioning of the house and the organization of the different interior spaces.

The residence is constructed entirely out of wood. Local artisans carefully placed each piece to fit with precision. Vegetation conceals a large part of the ground floor, and the visitor first perceives two small cabins with straw ceilings painted blue. In reality, these cabins, which merge with the tones of the sky and sea, belong to the upper floor of this enormous house. The residence's large dimensions seem lighter due to the use of local materials that reflect the typical architecture of the region.

The structure of the house reveals the family's needs. The client's requirements were crucial when it came to designing the project. The lot's proportions determined a succession of spaces that are open yet protected from the wind. The habitable rooms are dispersed in three different parts: one for guests, another for the children and a third for the parents.

After crossing the entrance, the first open space contains a heated pool that is linked to the guest rooms on one side and to the children's quarters on the other. On the ground floor, glass doors connect the children's living area to the exterior. The living room and the dining room are accompanied by a large kitchen that is connected to the exterior.

Architect: Mario Connio

Location: Punta Piedras, Punta del Este, Uruguay

Area: 10,752 sq. feet

Construction date: 1997

Photographer: Ricardo Labougle

This large house recalls the regional architecture and makes the most of its location by creating interior and exterior spaces protected from the strong winds.

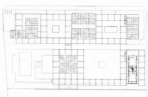

General plan

Module plan

The house is organized around open spaces that are protected from the wind by different modules. Each module contains a different residential space and function, which in turn relate to the exterior terraces.

The wood is painted white in the interior to create the sensation of luminosity and space without compromising the quality of the material. The structure of the roof is exposed, and its modulation and texture enrich the interior.

Conversion of a Stable

Marques ° Zurkirchen

The stable in Bergün, a town in Switzerland's Graubünden region, was to be refitted into a home was a massive stone-column construction. The mortised larch roof and ceiling architecture included a system of wooden pulley blocks for hauling. The project retained the original natural stone columns as well as the roof's solid old truss system. The natural protection of the region's traditional architecture would now be used for a new single-family unit.

The novelty of the construction lay largely in the new technologies used and the decorative devices, with the new larch bay fitting precisely into the old stone and protruding toward the town square. It was built with what was most available in the town itself: wood, with thermal insulation for the needs of this type of low-energy consumption house. The timbering includes an air chamber and galvanized sheet metal elements.

The encounter between the extant frame and the new bay develops on different levels. The use of indigenous materials infuses the project with a traditional spirit, creating a dialogue that includes the renewal of exterior spaces such as balconies and loggias. When all is said and done, great respect has been shown for the original building.

The interface between the different façades brings the massive masonry of the large windowed planes of the old stable together with the echoed motifs in the prefab wood-frame. Thus do tradition and modernity define the next decade's building concepts.

Architect: Marques ° Zurkirchen
Location: Bergün. Switzerland
Construction Date: 1994
Photographs: Ignacio Martinez

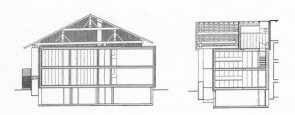

The new form was built with something available in the town itself: wood, with thermal insulation for the needs of this type of low-energy consumption house.

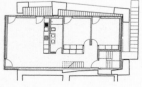

Access level

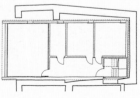

First floor

The area beneath the roof

The orientation of the new part of the stable onto the town's original setting contributes to the powerful value of the building in its urban context.

The mural features of this old stable were rata**ined during the conversion and refitting.

The interiors of the new addition were designed according to current needs, without reference to its rural origins.

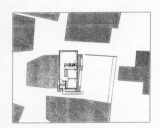

Site plan

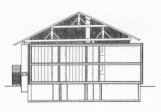

Longitudinal section

Cross section

The use of different materials to finish the walls contributes to the modern image of the dwelling. It also distinguishes, without the need of partitions, the different rooms.

The new duplex construction, faced in wood, has been set out from the main body, marke by the eave line of the building's hip roof. The convergence of the new part and the older, cleary rural part accentuates the contrast between the two concepts in the traditional town.

One of the façades of the building, perhaps the most urban, is separated from the street grade by scarcely more than three feet and including a light metal stairway. The whole building is intentionally isolated from its settings in this way.

Kaufmann House

Hermann Kaufmann

This home the tiny region of Vorarlberg, in northern Austria, consists of two sections placed perpendicularly on a slight slope. The socle acts as a transition between the domestic spaces and the lot and is dug partially into the ground. It houses the garage, several service rooms, and a storage area.

The upper level, perpendicular to the slope, is long and rises above the solid block like a balcony reaching out toward the magnificent Austrian countryside. This floor, which includes all the domestic rooms, is accessed by narrow wooden stairs supported by metal cylinders which are anchored in the framework of the upper level and also serve as handrails.

The northern, eastern, and western facades were constructed with boards made from three layers of larch wood, guaranteeing good thermal isolation. The joints between the boards are covered with long aluminum sheets that keep the building watertight. The southern façade, almost entirely glass, is protected by sliding blinds installed a short distance from the large windows. The space in between functions as a small balcony.

The roofs of the two sections are basically flat, with a slight slope for drainage. A fine covering of gravel and earth conceals the asphalt and insulating material. The local climate has encouraged the growth of a layer of grass, making the roof blend in with the landscape. Inside, the vertical surfaces are covered with wood, the typical finish of houses in the region.

Architect: **Hermann Kaufmann**
Collaborators: **Stefan Hiebeler and Anton Kaufmann**
Construction date: **1998**
Location: **Reuthe, Austria**
Area: **3900 sq. feet**
Photographs: **Ignacio Martinez**

Despite its contemporary design, the house, built into the ground and making heavy use of wood, blends in with the magnificent landscape.

Western Elevation

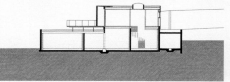

Cross-Section

Southern elevation

The owner of the house was also the builder. His lumber company provided the material and furnished specific information about complicated construction details.

The staircase is a magnificent piece of construction. Thin metal cylinders anchored in the framework of the upper level support the wooden stairs, which also rest on a steel column.

1. Garage - 2. Storage areas - 3. Office
4. Laundry room - 5. Walk-in closet
6. Bathrooms - 7. Corridor - 8. Kitchen
9. Study - 10. Living room - 11. Bedroom
12. Sauna

Innfeld House

Dietrich ○ Untertrifaller Architekten

The Innfeld House sits on the edge of a high plateau on the outskirts of the small Austrian town of Schwarzenberger. No garden was planned, so the cultivated land comes right up to the building's foundation. From the outset, the design process was influenced by the project's location. The designers wanted to make the most of the views of the surrounding valleys and the forests. So they planned a house whose upper level is almost transparent, with windows covering two thirds of the façade, and a large balcony, which is covered by the gabled roof.

At the rear of the house, facing northeast, three walls protect the private areas from the wind and cold. Just one sliding window and the access door break the thermal inertia of these solid walls. The outer walls are covered with larch siding. The narrowness of the wooden strips and the fact that they come right to the corners of the building give the impression of a continuous flat surface, light and transpirable, concealing the bearing structure.

The traditional layout of household functions is reversed to ensure that the common areas enjoy the best views of the landscape. The bedrooms, on the ground floor, also have windows, but they are smaller and don't enjoy the same views. Inside, the dark walnut floors contrast with the white walls and pale yellow of the pine woodwork. This heterogeneous combination of materials creates a warm, comfortable atmosphere conducive to relaxation and enjoyment of the scenery.

Architect: Dietrich ○ Untertrifaller Architekten
Collaborators: Marina Hämmerle
Construction date: 1999
Location: Schwarzenberger, Austria
Area: 3700 sq. feet
Photographs: Ignacio Martinez

Throughout the project, the structural skeleton is concealed: the gabled roof is supported by the walls at the rear of the house and by slender posts on the balcony, so it seems to be magically suspended above the domestic spaces.

The placement of the lower-ground floor ensures that no room is without light. This level houses the utility rooms, the laundry room, and a storage area, and insulates the rest of the house from humidity.

The balcony, with exceptional views of the charming Voralberg area, has wood flooring. The rails are an extension of the outer walls, supported on slender posts anchored to the structure.

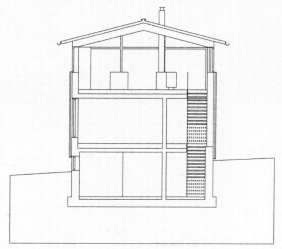

Cross Section

The living room, kitchen, and dining room occupy a single continuous space, which is dominated by the view of the scenery outside. Thanks to the enormous windows, the domestic spaces are flooded with natural light all day long. The kitchen furnishings were designed specifically for the project.

1. Laundry room - 2. Bedrooms - 3. Bathrooms
4. Master bedroom - 5. Living room - 6. Kitchen
7. Dining room - 8. Balcony

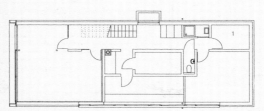

Lower-ground floor

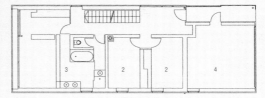

Ground floor

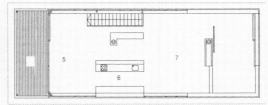

Second floor

To contrast with the dark tones of the walnut flooring, most of the vertical surfaces are white or made of translucent glass, which allows light to enter without sacrificing privacy.

Piu House

Tonet Sunyer

The Piu house project is located on the highway between Vic and Tavernoles, in the province of Barcelona. The building was placed far back on the lot, in a straight line, supported on three platforms that adjust for the unevenness of the land. The lowest level includes five stables for horses, while the living quarters were installed on the highest part of the lot.

The road leading to the house crosses the plot lengthwise, avoiding the slope, and divides the lot into two areas at different elevations: one for the horses, and the other, for the domestic areas, which was landscaped. In the future, a wall will enclose the swimming pool, the parking area, and the guest quarters, which are on the middle platform.

The residence, stables, and garage are sheltered by a pergola that unifies the grouping horizontally and provides shade along the entire length of the structure. These small terraces create an intermediate space between the interior and the outdoors.

The swimming pool is perpendicular to the house, parallel to the access road. Rows of black poplars were planted in front of the house.

The plan consists of two linear strips: on the northern side are the service areas, such as the kitchen and bathrooms; and on the southern side, the living room, dining room, and bedrooms. The master bedroom is located at one end and has an adjoining bathroom and ample dressing room.

Architect: Tonet Sunyer
Collaborator: Eduardo Doce
Construction date: 1997
Location: Vic, Spain
Area: 2365 sq. feet
Photographs: Eugeni Pons

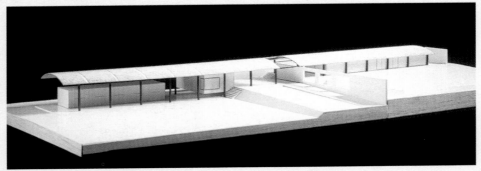

The master bedroom is located at one end and enjoys views in two directions. To filter the light and preserve the intimacy of the interior, the windows were covered with wooden slats.

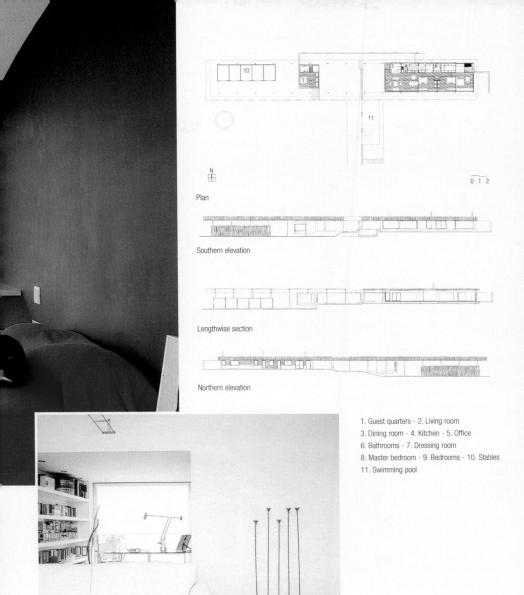

Plan

Southern elevation

Lengthwise section

Northern elevation

1. Guest quarters - 2. Living room
3. Dining room - 4. Kitchen - 5. Office
6. Bathrooms - 7. Dressing room
8. Master bedroom - 9. Bedrooms - 10. Stables
11. Swimming pool

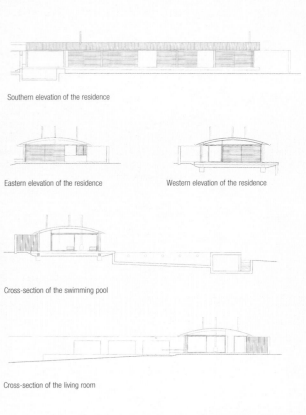

Southern elevation of the residence

Eastern elevation of the residence

Western elevation of the residence

Cross-section of the swimming pool

Cross-section of the living room

The living room is at the other end of the residence, adjoining a porch that leads to the swimming pool. This connection with the exterior heightens the feeling of spaciousness in the common areas.

House in Italy

Döring Dahmen Joeressen Architekten

This rural home sits on top of a small hill in the Italian countryside. After a careful geological survey due the the locations's subjectivity to earthquakes, the decision was made to build a reinforced concrete frame covered by brick walls to ensure rigidity. This supporting system is arranged on a 5 meter grid which dictates the layout of the house.

The brick walls are covered by blocks of native tufa. The porosity of this volcanic material gives the solid, heavy structure an ethereal quality. Also, the thickness of the pieces, 25 cm., makes for 65 cm. walls, enabling the builder to install shutters, a real necessity in Mediterranean climate. The thickness of the walls increase the building's thermal inertia, keeping it cool in summer and distributing the heat in the winter months.

The lower of the two levels contains an office and the rooms devoted to farming activities. The upper level, part of which, due to the slope of the land, is at ground level, contains the domestic spaces and a large terrace.

One of the goals of the design was to minimize the construction details. Expert local artisans were engaged to help solve certain technical problems.

The severe shapes and profusion of right angles contrast with the curved shapes of the surrounding natural world and the organic structures Bernhard Korte placed in the garden. The two pines that were already on the site now coexist with beautifully-shaped olive trees, all personally selected by Korte.

Architect: **Döring Dahmen Joeressen Architekten**
Collaborator: **Bernhard Korte**
Construction date: **2000**
Location: **Italy**
Area: **4300 sq. feet**
Photographs: **Manos Meisen**

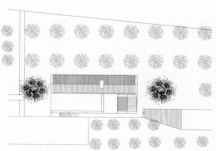

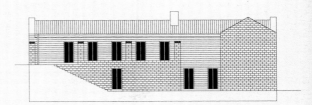

Southern elevation

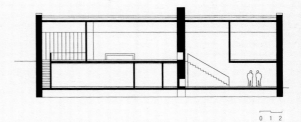

Lengthwise section

0 1 2

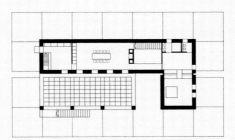

First floor

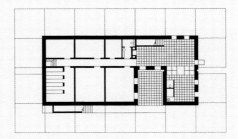

Second floor

Eastern elevation

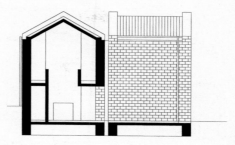

Cross-section

The interior spaces are just as unadorned as the exterior of the building. Right angles and simple geometric shapes dominate spaces illuminated through small openings in the solid walls.

Danielson House

Brian MacKay-Lyons

The Danielson house is a small refuge, designed as a place to stay for short periods of time. Two factors greatly influenced the project's design: the professions of the clients, a meteorologist and a landscape architect, and the impressive location of the site.

The residence sits at the edge of a small cliff and is surrounded by the typical forest found on the coast of Nova Scotia, in the extreme east of Canada. The composition is organized along a longitudinal wooden platform that is parallel to the line of the sea. A smaller building, attached to the wooden platform, contains storage, while a larger one, placed above the platform, contains the rest of the functions.

The interior scheme features the same simplicity as the general floor plan. The service and storage areas are grouped in the back part, which looks onto the forest. The living room is located on the other side and serves as an extension of the wooden platform inside. Two narrow wooden staircases lead to a loft above the service zone, which contains the sleeping quarters.

In order to keep costs down and take full advantage of the short construction period due to the seasons, the project was mostly prefabricated in Halifax. The technique of building a structure and then assembling it on the site comes from the legacy of boat construction, a traditional industry of the area. The refuge was also treated to endure the extreme climatic conditions of the zone.

Architect: Brian MacKay-Lyons Architecture
Collaborators: Bruno Weber, Trevor Davies, Darryl Jonas
Location: Smelt Brook, Nova Scotia, Canada
Area: 2,677 sq. feet
Completion date: 1998
Photographs: Undine Pröhl

This refined project has great spatial quality due to the clever contrast of three elements: a wooden platform and two light volumes.

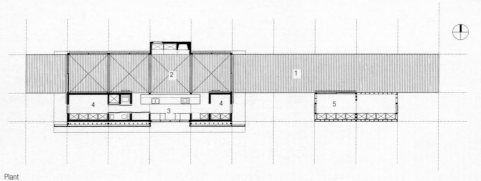

Plant

The isolation of the house, in the middle of a pine forest and at the high part of a cliff, made it impossible to closely link the interior and the exterior. The longitudinal wooden terrace is the principal element of the cabin's composition.

1. Terrace - 2. Living room - 3. Kitchen
4. Fixtures - 5. Storage

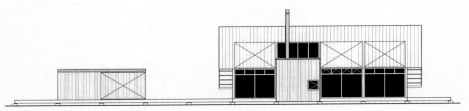

Elevation

Transversal section

A composition of wooden panels creates a solid element that breaks the transparency of the north façade. This area includes a chimney, some closets and a built-in sofa that complements the living room furnishings and enjoys the view through a small window.

House in Cavalli Beach

Chris Howe Architect

The owners of this residence located on a remote bay in the north of New Zealand, asked the architect to design a low-budget project that would have the minimum possible impact on the environment. The architect's objective, therefore, was to create a home that would balance comfort, design and vernacular references. The result is an object in the form of a shell that hugs the curve of the hill, relating to both the hill and the sea.

The construction is supported by 60 wooden pillars. The owners reforested the terrain surrounding the house with native trees and exotic palms, which make reference to the area's Polynesian origins. The three levels that make up the building are placed under the curved plane of the continuous roof, which was constructed using wooden, laminated beams. On the lower level, there are three bedrooms and bathrooms for guests, which open onto the wooden terrace toward the north, capturing the dramatic view of the bay. On the middle level, a glass-fronted living area links the interior with another wooden terrace. The upper level contains the master bedroom, bathroom and a small private study.

The architect carefully selected the interior and exterior details and materials in order to keep costs down and to create a dialogue with the history of the setting. Inside, the pillars are tied with linen fabrics produced by the Maori, who also made the rugs. The wood used inside the house and for the structure is radiated pine, a popular variety of the region.

Architect./designer: **Chris Howe**
Collaborators **Martyn Evans Architects**
Location: **Rapaki Beach, Northland, Nueva Zelanda**
Area: **4.734 sp. feet**
Construction date: **1998**
Photographs: **Patrick Reynolds y Chris Howe**

This project pays homage to the rich diversity of the area, including its Polynesian origins, the first European settlers, the local Maori culture and its current touristic image.

Ground floor

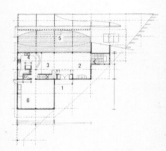

Second floor

First floor

1. Entrance - 2. Living room - 3. Dining room
4. Kitchen - 5. Terrace - 6. Parking
7. Main Bedroom - 8. Studio - 9. Bedroom
10. Children´s studio

Elevation

A continual roof, supported on both extremes of the terrain, is the most important element of the project's composition. The openings towards the exterior terraces enjoy views of the bay and reveal their wooden structure.

The sliding doors that compose the back façade leave the interior space free, connecting it directly with the longitudinal terrace that crosses the house. The wood furnishings complement the exposed structure and the exterior details, made of the same material.

House in Bay of Islands

Pete Bossley Architect

This vacation house is a family refuge set in the Bay of Islands, in the northern part of New Zealand. In honor of the setting, the building emphasizes and enriches the island experience.

The project is a large composition of elements that were constructed on the mainland and assembled on the island. The search for a precise and structurally expressive architectural language inspired the architect to create the home out of wood, the material par excellence in New Zealand. Bossley also explored the influence of the Group Architects, who became national legends in the mid-twentieth century.

Many settlements in New Zealand are located in transitional zones along the coasts. Most houses built on the bays tend to follow the colonial tradition which placed the building in the center of the lot. This residence differs in that it is located on the side of the land, under some existing trees. The luminosity of the house as well as the structure that sustains a large roof create a certain sense of temporariness, appropriate to a vacation home.

The construction used wooden applications that required great precision from fine artisans. The exterior walls feature carpentry from top to bottom, while the interior walls are covered with cedar panels to the height of the doors and then with glass to the ceiling. The 132-foot-long roof floats above the walls and is supported by a structure of slender wooden frames.

Architect: **Pete Bossley**
Collaborators: **James Downey, Andrea Bell, Don McKenzie**
Location: **Bay of Islands, New Zealand**
Surface: **3,163 square feet**
Date: **1997**
Photographer: **Patrick Reynolds**

This cabin embodies the process of construction and
composition and the balance between structure and
form, creating a sense of intimacy, richness and presence in the interior space.

Plan

⊗   1. Entrance - 2. Kitchen - 3. Dining room
    4. Living room - 5. Bedrooms

Elevation

Section

Due to the difficulty of constructing on the island, the house is made mostly of prefabricated elements that were assembled on the site. The structure is made entirely of wooden frames.

The linear layout follows a north-south axis, staggering the land on eight different levels clearly defined by structural wood frames that the walls leave free. The house's width is adjusted according to the needs of the rooms, which all have a view of the beach.

The Rock of las Hadas Island

Alberto Burckhardt

This project is located on a small island, composed of two small cays that form part of the Archipelago Natural Park on the Rosario Islands, in Colombia. Having deteriorated after years of abandonment, a planning process started with a global concept of the land. The architect consolidated the existing elements and incorporated new architectural elements to create a recreational residence.

The project's main challenge was to transform an existing house, a composition with modern lines, into a building appropriate for the Caribbean atmosphere. Preserving the basic structure of the house, the architect carefully studied the openings to give the interior spaces a 360-degree view of the site.

Special features of the project include the pergolas that filter the light, the rattan rails with ties, wooden terraces that extend the interior space, and flexible closures that fully integrate the volume with its surroundings. The house, the kiosk and the jetties highlight the work in macana and teak, woods of high quality and resistance from the Caribbean region.

The project includes two two-story modules located on the two cays that make up the small island, which are separated by a channel of water. A teak platform placed above the channel integrates the living room in the southern module with the dining room and the services in the northern module. A staircase continues to the roof where there is a terrace-lookout that provides spectacular views of the surrounding landscape.

Architect: Alberto Burckhardt
Location: Rosario Islands. Colombia
Area: 12.900 sq. feet
Construction date: 1999
Photographs: Silvia Patiño

This project entailed the construction of a recreational residence as well as the recovery of a small island and its structures, which had deteriorated after years of abandonment.

This house is set on two small islands. The elements that define the islands are an integral part of the residence, including the stone barriers and the native vegetation. As a result of the environment, the house's design closely links the interior and the exterior.

Two wood piers, the only way to access the house, stretch out on the northern and southern sides like outdoor extensions of the house. The arrangement towards the south creates a close-up view, in an attempt to capture an image of the sea, creating diverse visual relationships with a minimal gesture.

1. Entrance - 2. Living room - Dining room / Kitchen - 3. Bedrooms - 4. Guest house

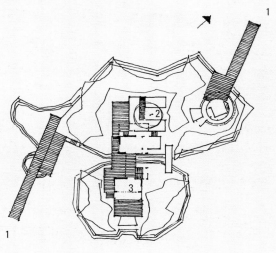

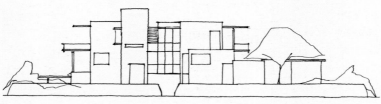

Elevation

Despite the solidity of the structure and the exterior façades, the house has a permanent relationship with the exterior due to a succession of open but covered spaces, exterior terraces and a distant view of the horizon and the sea.

An outstanding feature of the interior is the artisan work in macana, a wood typical of the Caribbean region which was used for the construction of the roof, the rails of the staircase and the details of the furnishings.

The guest house is composed of a circular volume, in the form of a kiosk, that is totally isolated from the main house. The module contains a living area, a bedroom and a bathroom.

Berk Rauch Residence

Stelle Architects

This summer house is located on the southern part of Long Island in New York. While the setting includes magnificent beaches, it's also a zone of high density and urban development due to its proximity to big cities and its popularity as a recreational area. The configuration of the landscape creates some nearby views, as if they were small gardens, in contrast to the open panorama of the ocean. This project responds to this context by providing shelter and privacy from the immediate neighbors. The house also opens itself to the Atlantic on the southern part of the property.

The clients' needs inspired the architect to design a scheme of three different volumes: a wing for the parents, another for the children and a third with a living and family zone. In each module, the architect designed a unique, continual space with a close relationship to the exterior. The volumes' configuration in a rotary sense creates an intense interaction between the blocks, yet permits them to have their own character and privacy. The exterior space is shaped by terraces and by the volumes themselves.

Inside, the structure and the exposed elements reflect the lightness of the construction. The columns and beams, in soft colors, reinforce the architect's intention to create a tranquil and fresh atmosphere. In contrast, the exterior part is covered with more solid materials like cedar and concrete to protect the house against the abrasive effects of the wind, salt and sand.

Architect: Stelle Architects
Collaborators: Frederick Stelle, Walter Wilcoxen, Alexander Keller
Location: Sea View, Fire Island, United States
Area: 4.000 sq. feet
Construction date: 2000
Photographs: Jeff Heatley

This project manages with few gestures and an
austere, formal language, to integrate harmo-
niously with the surrounding landscape and to
create a tranquil interior space.

The wooden pillars that support the house also serve as a leveling system that places the building lightly above the landscape of dunes and rugged vegetation. This design also prevents the accumulation of sand in times of strong winds.

The structural elements of the house are exposed and form part of the cozy, calm interior atmosphere along with the floors, window frames and dividing panels.

The service areas are treated with simplicity, emphasizing the house's relaxed and informal character. The kitchen, at the back of the living area, is integrated with the dining room. Both share a large table that has two levels.

1. Entrance - 2. Dining room - 3. Kitchen
4. Studio - 5. Main room - 6. Bedrooms
7. Terrace - 8. Swimming pool

Ground floor

Mezzanine

Lutz House

David Salmela

This house is situated along a lake near Duluth, Minnesota, in an area where Swedish immigrant families who retained the custom of enjoying a second residence far from the urban hustle and bustle used to spend their summers. The family owned the original building, which was in poor condition and was torn down. The foundations and the old fireplace were retained for sentimental reasons, and the new house was built behind them, closer to the water.

The building is long and narrow, with magnificent views and abundant natural light. It consists of a cube that houses several rooms on two floors, and a two-story living room. The rooms are open and can be used for different purposes.

The exterior spaces were carefully designed for enjoyment of outdoor activities. There are two routes to the lake: around the ruins or directly from the house, across a porch that provides shade in the summer.

The house's wooden structure is supported by a system of concrete pillars that raise it above ground level, protecting it from dampness. The exterior walls are cedar and painted plywood, and the interior is pine. Some of the furnishings, like those in the kitchen, and most of the closets, are built into the walls. Out of a deep concern for the ecology, the architect and clients made sure that no materials harmful to the environment were used.

The electrical and mechanical systems were installed between the floor and the ground, so they would be accessible but out of the way of any household activity.

Architect: **David Salmela**
Construction date: **1998**
Location: **Duluth, Minnesota, USA**
Area: **1095 sq. feet**
Photographs: **Peter Kerze**

1. Bedroom - 2. Kitchen - 3. Living room
4. Bathroom - 5. Bedroom - 6. Bathroom
7. Two-story space - 8. Study

Plan of the original house   First floor   Second floor

The house has contemporary architectural lines with subtle classical references. It is both rustic and unconventional. These recurring paradoxes make for an interesting project, full of feeling.

The interior reflects the owners' artistic interests: music, painting, and ceramics.

Eastern elevation

Northern elevation

Western elevation

Southern elevation

Wood Residence

James Cutler Architects

The Wood residence is protected by the trees of a lush forest on its northern side, but is exposed on the southern side to take advantage of the clearing's light and views.

Enormous effort was required to satisfy the clients' needs and deal with the features of the land. James Cutler is known for respecting the sites on which he builds, so an important part of the design was an in-depth study of the climate and special characteristics of the plot. In this case, the position of the house and the layout of the rooms were determined by the search for natural light and the desire to retain the existing trees, which stand right near the house.

The residence is comprised of several structures connected by a back hallway that runs its entire length, leveling the slight slopes and leading out to the forest. So the units containing the bedrooms, dayroom, laundry room, greenhouse, and garage are all lined up. The stable and the granary are located a few meters from the residence.

The predominant building material is wood: the vertical interior partitions are panels of pine, the flooring is maple, and the exterior walls are covered with cedar shingles. The only significant amount of metal is in the roof, which is a series of galvanized metal strips. Cutler's dexterity and precision in working the wood are magnificent. The details are visible throughout, and the finishes and structural elements are a lesson in construction in and of themselves.

Architect: James Cutler Architects
Construction date: 1997
Location: Vashon Island, Washington, USA
Area: 2320 sq. feet
Photographs: Undine Pröh

Elevation

The interior is all wood. The furniture, designed by the architects - note the kitchen cupboards and the living room cabinets - were conceived as self-contained modules. Lighting was installed above the furnishings and below the ceiling.

Erlandson Villa

Per Friberg Arkitektbyrå

The Erlandson villa sits in a forest clearing. The unique location of the plot determined the architects' and clients' requirements. The surrounding natural setting could not be altered for the house. Also, the domestic spaces had to take advantage of the natural light offered by the absence of trees in the immediate vicinity of the structure.

The house was built on a wooden platform to protect it from the damp Nordic climate. This strategy makes almost no difference in the overall appearance, other than enhancing the sense of lightness. The ethereal quality of the facades and interior partitions emphasizes this effect.

The layout is fairly conventional: the common rooms are on the first floor and the private rooms are on the upper floor, which also includes a generous balcony that offers views of the surrounding area. The hall and stairs were placed on the north side to avoid blocking the warm light entering from the south.

The predominant building material is wood, in deference to the concepts of ecology and comfort on which the design process was based. The framework consists of an orthogonal system of beams and posts that support the different parts of the building. The exterior walls are supported by vertical wooden uprights that also form the window frames. The construction details were carefully designed and remain visible to enhance the house's bright, solid appearance. This is especially apparent in the junctures of the structural elements or the eaves boards.

Architect: Per Friberg Arkitektbyrå
Construction date: 1999
Location: Ljunghusen, Sweden
Area: 2470 sq. feet
Photographs: Åke E: Son Lindman

The house and terraces sit on a platform, supported by posts, a few centimeters above the ground.

The balconies and terraces surrounding the Erlandson villa are made of wooden strips with a few millimeters of space between them to let the daylight shine through and give the building a light, ethereal look.

The designers decided to place the stairs that connect the two floors alongside the rectangular residence. They do not take up space that could be otherwise used or interfere with household activities.

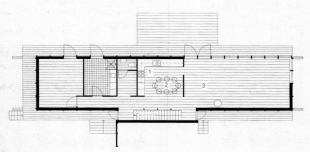

Second floor

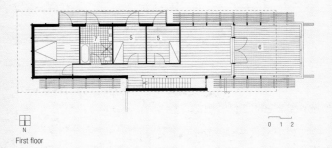

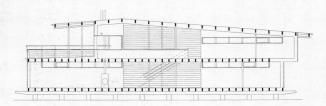

N

0 1 2

First floor

Section

1 Kitchen - 2 Dining room - 3 Living room
4 Master bedroom - 5 Bedrooms
6 Terrace - 7 Bathroom

The interior and exterior walls are made entirely of wood. The living room has abundant glass for natural light and views of the garden. The furniture includes specially-designed pieces.

Hanson House

David Salmela

The location of the house, right on top of a rocky mass adjoing Quetico Provincial Park, was determined by US laws requiring buildings to be at least 50 meters back from the lakefront. The structure is built around a courtyard that includes the highest rock, making it the heart of the grouping.

The plan called for a dayroom and abundant sleeping space, inasmuch as the home will be a gathering place for the entire family during vacations. The living room, kitchen, and dining room face the lake and the central courtyard. For privacy, the bedrooms were placed in a loft and in the northern wing. This isolation does not keep the bedrooms from enjoying abundant natural light and views of the surroundings.

A small storehouse placed apart from the grouping is reminiscent of the old barns found on local farms.

A platform resting on concrete pillars supports the wooden beams and posts of the framework. The courtyard walls were inspired by Alvar Aalto's Muuratsalo house in Finland, but in this project the walls are strips of painted or varnished wood rather than brick.

The brilliance of this project lies in having taken the rocky mass, which at first was the main obstacle to construction, and made it the focal point of the grouping, around which all the rooms of the house are arranged. Moreover, the project combines the qualities of the old wooden cabins with modern layouts that take advantage of the views and natural light.

Architect: **David Salmela**
Construction date: **1997**
Location: **Northeastern Minnesota, USA**
Area: **1590 sq. feet**
Photographs: **Peter Kerze**

At the clients' request, David Salmela surrounded
the house with porches. Each is made of different
quarterings of wooden planks.

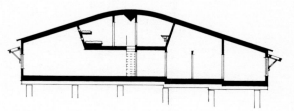

The measurements had to be very precise, because the rough terrain meant that many of the elements would be in direct contact with the rock. Each of the stairs to the house is a different length, to fit the space between the building and the rock.

1 Entrance - 2 Living room - 3 Porch
4 Laundry room - 5 Bathroom
6 Dressing room - 7 Bedrooms - 8 Loft
9 Offices - 10 Storehouse

First floor

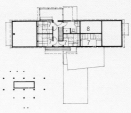

N   Second floor   0 1 2

Although it sits amid the lush woods, the house, situated on the crest of a hill, is visible from various points.

The construction details demonstrate the architect's expertise with wood. The joinings of the framework and the facades, the window frames and the staircase, are magnificent examples of a good artisan's skill.

Site plan

Section

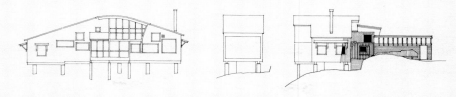

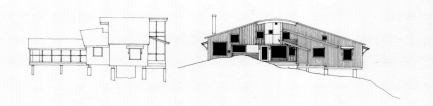

Elevations

Most of the furniture is built in. The closets, some sofas, and the many beds were made of wood, just for the project. This strategy unifies the grouping and provides comfort and convenience.

House on Mount Fuji

Satoshi Okada

This house is located at the base of Mount Fuji, in an area of thick vegetation boasting many trees. The peacefulness and isolation of the beech and birch forests is broken only by a nearby cabin. For architect Satoshi Okada, this project was a poetic exercise. The building is like a monument, a structure that is solid but camouflaged amid the foliage, a "shadow in the forest," according to Okada.

The clients commissioned this small weekend home so they could enjoy the tranquility of the location with their guests. The building was situated in the northeastern corner of the lot, to take advantage of the abundant natural light and still remain private. A roof with multiple slopes is in harmony with the uneven terrain.

A large diagonal wall divides the house into two segments: a spacious area housing the common domestic functions, and another area for the bedrooms and bathrooms. At the entrance, a long corridor widens to become an enormous gallery illuminated by light from above. This space contains a kitchen and dining room underneath a lowered 6.5 foot ceiling and a living room underneath a high, 16.5 foot ceiling. A small hall leads to the bedrooms.

Like the architectural forms, the materials chosen harmonize with the peaceful surroundings. So wood is used throughout. The façade is cedar stained black, and the floor is covered with oak parquet. For reasons of practicality, the bathroom and terrace floors are granite.

Architect: **Satoshi Okada**
Collaborators: **Lisa Tomiyama and Eisuke Aida**
Construction date: **2000**
Location: **Narusawa Village, Japan**
Area: **1480 sq. feet**
Photographs: **Hiroyuki Hirai**

The building is clearly outlined under the treetops and above the lava it attempts to emulate. The house is accessed by means of a short ramp that bridges the gap between the ground and the entrance, which are at two different levels.

Southeast elevation

Southwest elevation

Northwest elevation

Northeast elevation

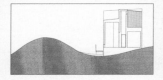

Cross-section

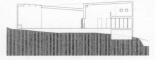

Lengthwise section

At some points the façade appears to be an impregnable wall, but at others, the sections are differentiated and the arrangement of the interior domestic space is revealed.

The exterior walls are set back at certain points to shape terraces that afford views of the surroundings and provide an enclave for outdoor living. Overhangs provide protection from inclement weather.

There are few doors inside. Rooms are delimited by gaps in the walls and light entering from above.

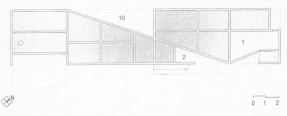

First floor

Second floor

Third floor

1. Storage area - 2. Machine room - 3. Ramp
4. Entrance - 5. Living room - 6. Hall
7. Tatami room - 8. Terrace - 9. Balcony
10. Patio - 11. Bedroom - 12. Loft
13. Empty space - 14. Roof

Arketorp Villa
Erik Stähl

The lot chosen for this single-family home is located in a rural area just 7 kilometers from the heart of the small city of Jönköping. The spectacular views of a forest of oak trees and nearby Lake Vättern make the spot truly unique.

Great care was taken to save the existing trees and keep the natural surroundings intact. No artificial garden was planned, other than arranging the plants on the patio at the entrance to resemble a Japanese garden, but adapted to Swedish culture and personal preferences.

The building is fully in tune with the architect's exquisite sensitivity to nature. Accordingly, he sought a close relationship between the interior and the outdoors, especially to enhance enjoyment of the landscape during the longed-for Swedish summer. One can savor views of the surrounding plant life from anywhere in the house.

The house is organized around a central corridor from which two small halls branch off. These connect all the rooms. This system of passages affords multiple connections and creates many meeting places, small vestibules in front of all the rooms, that enhance relationships among the residents.

The natural light and the choice of materials emphasize the concept of the project as a home surrounded by nature. Birch plywood is the predominant material for the walls and ceilings. In stark contrast, the door and window frames were painted dark brown. In the small bedrooms the floor is beechwood, and in the rest of the house, the flooring is ceramic glass.

Architect: **Erik Stähl**
Collaborators: **Erik Persson and Rolf Almqvist**
Construction date: **2000**
Location: **Jönköping, Sweden**
Area: **5100 sq. feet**
Photographs: **Jan Erik Ejenstam and Erik Stähl**

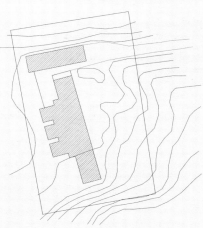

Different surfaces around the house mark the transition between plant life and building. At some points, small wooden terraces were built. Gravel was spread in front of the private areas to discourage passers-by. Different levels are joined by sturdy stairs of exposed concrete.

The exterior is covered with pine. The wood was pressure treated to protect it from the ravages of climate and insects. The exterior window and door frames were painted dark brown.

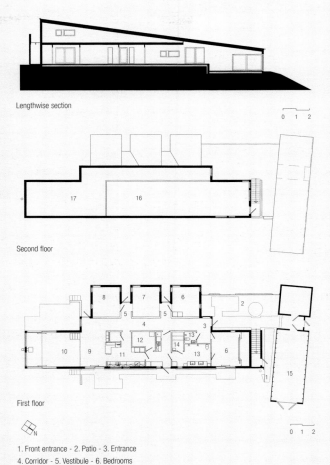

Lengthwise section

0 1 2

Second floor

First floor

N

0 1 2

1. Front entrance - 2. Patio - 3. Entrance
4. Corridor - 5. Vestibule - 6. Bedrooms
7. Living room - 8. Study - 9. Dining room
10. Living Room - 11. Kitchen
12. Walk-in closet - 13. Bathrooms
14. Sauna - 15. Garage - 16. Storage area
17. Terrace

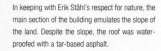

In keeping with Erik Ståhl's respect for nature, the main section of the building emulates the slope of the land. Despite the slope, the roof was water-proofed with a tar-based asphalt.

Kvarnhuset Villa

Wingårdh Arkitektkontor

The Kvarnhuset Villa project consisted of converting a mill into a weekend home. The property, originally part of a farm, is in a small town outside MalmöThe house, which is the work of a team headed by Gert Wingardh, is the building nearest the stream and sits on a platform that juts out over a stream.

The standard living quarters were supplemented with a sauna. Therapeutic rituals like the sauna spawned additional spaces, including a room where users relax before entering the sauna and a swimming pool next to the house for taking cold baths at the end of each session. The living room, kitchen, bathroom, and sauna are on the first floor. Since it is surrounded by a terrace and closed off by sliding glass doors, the relationship with the exterior is intense, and the house's dominant position is enhanced. The bedroom is in the loft, which is accessed by a stairway at one end of the house. Because of its unusual location, under the sloping roof, it has two triangular walls, one wood and the other glass.

The furniture, designed by the architects themselves, is also wood. The walls and flooring are concrete and stone, and the exterior walls combine glass with wood trim. The roof is covered by a series of small pieces of slate that evoke the building's agricultural past. Despite the project's small size, care in the selection of materials and mastery of the construction details have produced a true architectural jewel.

Architect: Wingårdh Arkitektkontor
Collaborators: Gunnar Altenhammar and Dagon förvaltnings
Construction date: 2000
Location: Skåne, Sweden
Area: 1182 sq. feet
Photographes: Åke E:Son Lindman

Tradition requires that after a session in the sauna one take an icy dip. Since the stream that skirts the property was not big enough, a small swimming pool was installed next to the sauna.

Second floor

1. Living room - 2. Kitchen - 3. Bathroom
4. Sauna - 5. Bedroom

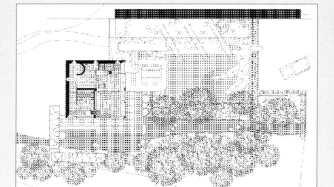

First floor

The bedroom is in the loft, a small space under the sloping roof. The northwestern facade has no windows and is finished with the same wood as the floor and ceiling. The southeastern facade is translucent glass with metal trim.

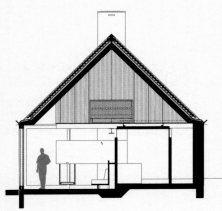

Section through the living rom

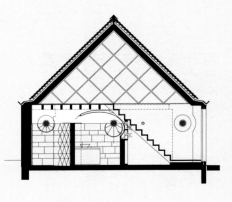

Section through the sauna

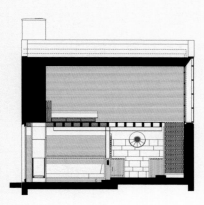

Section through the living room

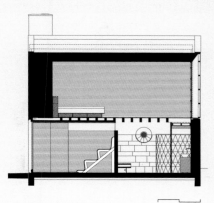

Section through the sauna

0   1   2

Jones House
David Salmela

The clients, who entrusted this project to David Salmela, had always lived in the city until, in their fifties, they decided to build a house in the country, and become farmers. The main objective was to design a farmstead adapted to the latest agricultural technology yet respectful of a traditional rural setting.

The owners' needs and desires included a granary, guest quarters, a residence, and a garage. All these structures had to be independent, appropriately linked, and optimally positioned to enjoy views of the countryside. Since one of the clients has limited mobility, the entire complex had to be accessible.

The granary is separate from the house, but both structures are covered by the same roof, which marks the limits of a south-facing courtyard. The house has an L-shaped design. The common areas are found in the long leg.

The couple's bedroom is located in the short leg, which also has a workroom, a swimming pool for therapy, and a laundry room. The cottage, on the other side of the courtyard, contains an office, guest rooms, and rooms for the machinery.

The forms David Salmela chose evoke the structures common to the area and blend with the countryside. He selected materials frequently used in local construction: brick, echoing the old silos; metal for the roofs and wood, especially cypress and fir. Far from appearing to be nostalgic contrivances, these elements give the complex a rural feel.

Architect: David Salmela
Collaborator: Souliyahn Keobounpheng
Construction date: 2000
Location: Nerstrand, Southern Minnesota, USA
Area: 6580 sq.feet
Photographs: Peter Kerze

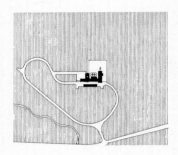

One of the main concerns of both the clients and the architect was the house's impact on its surroundings, so landscape architects Coen+Stumpf & Associates were hired to make sure the building harmonized with its natural setting.

The light sources are abundant: floor-to-ceiling windows, sliding doors leading to the courtyard, and small, strategically-placed openings to illuminate some of the rooms.

The interior is finished almost entirely in wood: cypress, pine, and painted plywood.

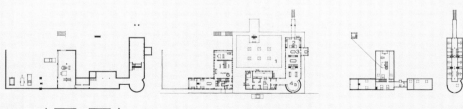

Lower ground floor

First floor

Second floor

1. Courtyard - 2. Kitchen - 3. Dining room

4. Living room - 5. Master bedroom

6. Guest quarters

The kitchen, like the rest of the house, has an old-fashioned feeling to it, evoking traditional rural homes, but it enjoys all the modern conveniences.

The stairs from the first floor to the loft are wood. Slender panels, painted white, with one end anchored to the framework above and the other to the stair treads, take the place of handrails.

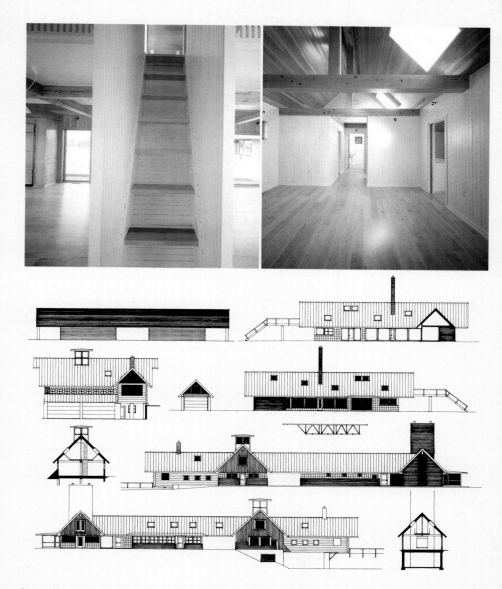

Sections and elevations

Yardbird Studio

Neal R. Deputy Architect Inc.

"Yardbird" is a small 270 sq. foot office that can be set up in the rear garden of any residence. Its function is to create a working space that remains isolated from the functions of the home.

This prototype is constructed in Charlottesville, Virginia (USA). A formal language characteristic of the area was consolidated by taking the classical european model and respecting local materials such as red brick, wood and metal roofing. The project opted for a classical scheme by searching for references to the context within the materials and the use of local construction techniques. Nevertheless, the design incorporates contemporary elements: steel windows, rigorous metal cladding and an exposed metallic base.

The volume is perceived as an elevated box covered in undulated metallic sheeting supported on metallic pillars anchored to a concrete base.
The openings in the front and lateral sides are constituted by a prefabricated system of folding aluminium windows.

Inside all the horizontal surfaces (pavement, tables and shelves) are finished in wood and rubber lining. The steel staircase, awnings, lights and storage systems are industrially prefabricated.

The project is vey simple: one bedroom (11.5 ft x 19.5 ft) elevated from the floor by way of pillars, giving the space a great independence and at the same time a better panorama. The metallic eave that envelops the corner window protects the interior space from the sun.

Architect: Neal R. Deputy • Gaither Pratt
Location: Charlottesville, Virginia, USA
Surface area: 269 sq. ft.
Date: 2000
Photographer: Jim Rounsevell

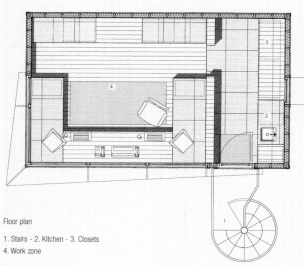

Floor plan

1. Stairs - 2. Kitchen - 3. Closets
4. Work zone

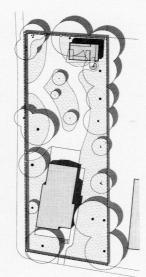

Site plan

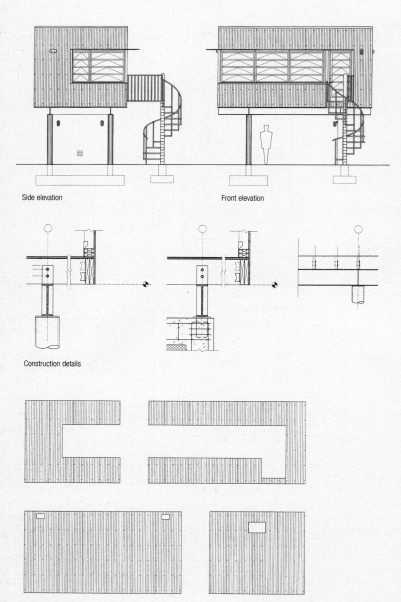

Side elevation

Front elevation

Construction details

Section scheme of metal sheeting

The shape and the dimensions of the space allow excellent interior flexibility. The project's distribution can be adapted to many different needs.

Oasis Apartments

Hans Peter Wörndl, Wolfgang Tschapeller, Max Rider

The SteinerstraBe, or Oasis apartments, consists of two housing blocks that contain 48 residences in Salzburg, Austria. Its appearance and aesthetic concept is still quite criticised by the surrounding neighborhood. The T-shape distribution of its rows of homes, its elastic film cladding and its image somewhere between industrial and domestic make this building stand out in the urban landscape of the city.

Lowering the level the the land to a reduced height was the first operation that made up the general scheme. This permitted the creation of a series of private gardens on the ground floor and the main access to remain on the level above.

The site is practically square and parallel to SteinerstraBe street. The project is configured around two entities that divide the site into two identical rectangles.

The relationship with the garden is emphasized by the wooden boxes that adhere to the longitudinal block, where the kitchen, access and bathroom of each apartment are located. The boxes also create a lateral wooden terrace that adds character to the façade.

A similar relationship with exterior is established on the upper floors, where the façade, which recedes at certain points, generates openings with the best panoramic views of the city.

On the top floor, the elastic membrane cladding offers the sensation of continuity. The fixed points of the membrane, which are established in two directions to cancel out the force of the wind, generates a perception of the façade as upholstered furniture.

Architect: Hans Peter Wörndl, Wolfgang Tschapeller, Max Rider
Location: Salzburg, Austria
Area: 37,674 sq. ft.
Construction date: 2001
Photographs: Paul Ott

The duplex apartment scheme includes exterior gardens and terraces. The finished product provides each unit with a character more like a detached house than an apartment in a series of clones.

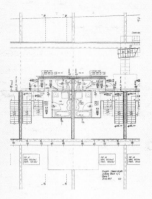

Floor plan

Longitudinal section

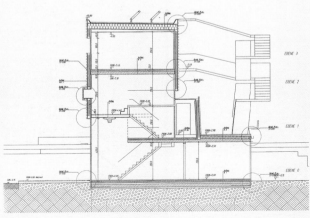

Transversal section

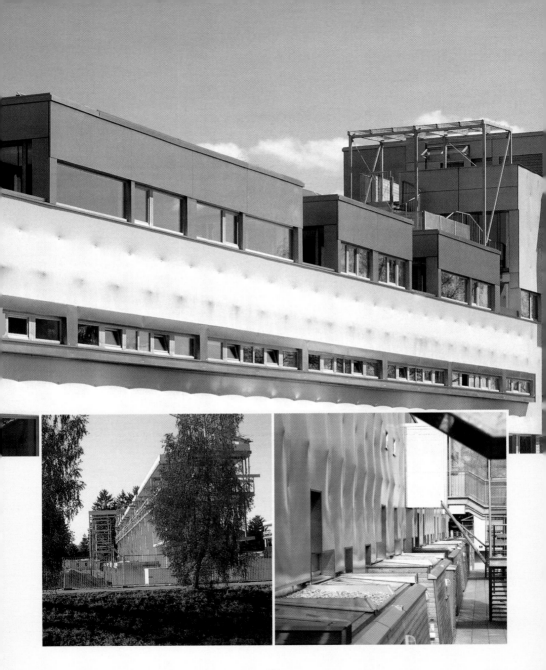

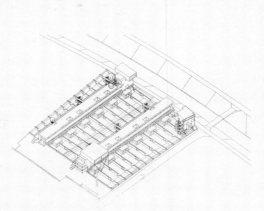

Aerial pespective

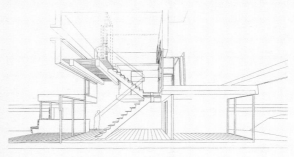

Section, a residence in perspective

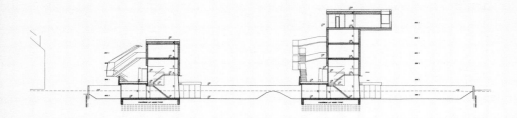

General transversal sections

The varied mix of materials like wood, elastic membrane, or metal panels, endow every nook and cranny of the place with its own character. This tailor-made feel is underscored by the fractionalization of the area and by its formal language.

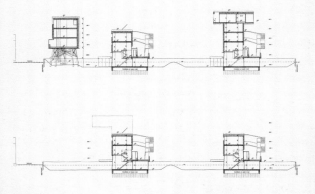

Burghalde

Alioth Langlotz Stalder Buol

The volume of the complex and its integration into the site respond to the division of the residences into identical spaces. This complex of four homes incorporates an additional structure on the lowere levels designated for occasional guests.

Situating the building on the highest part of the terrain allowed each home to dispose of street-level access and to enjoy panoramic views.

The block was constructed from prefabricated wooden pieces. The structural base is made up of metallic frames that rest on top of concrete slabs which serve to level-out the slope of the land. The remaining elements, inluciding the floors, walls, façades, doors and windows were produced off-site, transported and mounted in a minimum amount of time.

Each home is a module in which the same interior distribution is repeated. Located on the access level is a parking area, bathroom and open space which can be used alternatively as a bedroom or studio. Behind the main access, a stairwell leads to the lower and upper floor. The bedrooms, a bathroom and a washing room are located on the lower level where a set of stairs leads to a communal garden. The living room, dining room and kitchen share one single space on the upper level.

The use of wood, both in the structure and finishes, generate a project that combines a traditional and contemporary aesthetic.

Architect: Adriana Stalder ○ Leo Buol / Alioth Langlotz Stalder Boul
Collaborators: Thomas Henz, Philipp Esch
Location: Liestal, Switzerland
Area: 7,320 sq. ft.
Construction date: 1998
Photographs: Leo Buol

Floor plan of the complex

1. Access - 2. Parking
3. Bedroom/Studio - 4. Habitación - 5. Closet
6. Living/dinig room - 7. Kitchen - 8. Balcony

Back elevation

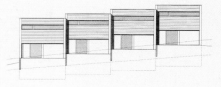

Interior elevation

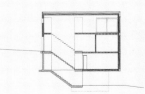

Transversal section

House G

Hans Gangoly

The house is based on a simple structural concept that makes the most of the conditions presented by the project. The small piece of land is flanked by neighboring buildings and has distant views towards the east and west.

The roof and mezzanine extend between the two glass façades and are supporte by a system of metal beams that run longitudinally. This produced a diaphanous interior.

The two façades are constructed from prefabricated frames and large glass panels. The frames are placed over the edges of the exterior walls. The large glass surfaces are partially covered by awnings to guarantee an adequate entry of light. The lower floor features a wooden terrace attached to the living and dining room which allows the space to open up onto the garden, making the most of a relatively small 1,205 sq. foot home. All the interior spaces circulate around this terrace. A monolithic staircase links the building with the street and leads into the homes. Inside, a staircase that runs along the façade leads to the first floor and a sculptural external stairwell provides access to the covered terrace. The projection of the front door defines the acess zone and circulation of spaces while the fireplace delineates the center of the living area. An L-shaped aperture relates the spaces in between the two levels.

Architect: **Hans Gangoly**
Location: **Graz, Austria**
Area: **1,237 sq. ft.**
Construction date: **1998**
Photographs: **Paul Ott**

The prefab framing system and ьnat of the glass wall create a free and independent composition that interrelates with the different proportions, both fixed and movable. The vertical awnings inside and outside interface with the upper sections of the house to create a nearly transparent adornment.

1. Access - 2. Kitchen - 3. Living/dinig room

This home, built in the rear garden of a 1930's house, was constructed in four months with solely prefabricated elements. It is composed of wooden frames that constitute the main structure, wooden fiber panels and metallic windows.

The project is based on two premises: to minimize the impact on the existing house and reduce as much as possible the area it occupies in the garden. The building can be simplified as a cubic object consisting of two floors and a contemporary aesthetic. The panels that make up the exterior and interior cladding were reduced to a minimal section to make the most of the space and to achieve greater thermal insulation.

The connection with the garden was executed by way of a large glass surface which defines the ground floor façade and from where a wooden terrace extends. A bridge on the upper floor unites the new volume with the existing house.

The façade is finished with cement and fiber slabs varnished in a grey-blue tone. The precise geometry of the building is emphasized by the grid formed by the junctions of the panels on the exterior façade. The openings are formed by grey-colored frames that are inserted at the same level as the paneles to reinforce the idea of a continuous cladding. On the upper level, the wood shutters protect the bedrooms from direct sunlight and the living, dining room and kitchen on the lower level open up to the exterior by way of sliding doors.

Architect: Christof Wallner
Collaborators: Bettina Görgner, Johana Kratzert, Patrick von Ridder
Location: Munich, Germany
Area: 1.345 sq. ft.
Construction date: 2000
Photographs: Michael Heinrich

Sección

1. Access - 2. Living room - 3. Kitchen/dinig room
4. Guest bathroom - 5. Main bedroom - 6. Bedroom
7. Bathroom - 8. Basement

Ground floor

Upper floor

The notable contrast between the new construction and the reformed element points up the way both living styles and building styles have changed.

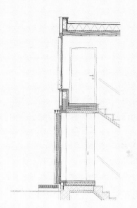

Basement plan

Façade detail

House Stockner

Wolfgang Feyferlık

This project designed as the second residence for a couple with children consists of two separate buildings: the main house and the other designated for guests. Only the latter building has been constructed so far.

The surrounding rural landscape and the concept of the building as a secondary structure led the architect to realize a lightweight volume that would not affect the setting. The prefabricated wooden frames constitute the structure of the house. The skeleton is lined with birch panels on the inside and rough laminas of fir tree wood on the outside. The roof is zinc and the south façade is divided into two parts, one distinguished by folding glass doors and the other by solar panels. The slight inclination of the land, which renders panoramic views over the valley, runs freely underneath the construction, which is slightly elevated from the ground.

Three sides of the house are practically closed, its main façade orientated towards the south and accessed from the east by a wooden walkway.

The floor distribution satisfies the needs of various individuals. Two nearly identical bedrooms are naturally lit and ventilated and accessed through a common area. This corridor, used as a kitchen and sitting area, links to either one or both of the rooms via sliding panels. The bathroom consists of a small booth wrapped in water-proof wood lining. Every inch of space is put to use in this small area. The suspended basin permits the water tank to be concealed behind a panel, allowing the space to breathe.

Architect: Wolfgang Feyferlık
Location: Tamach, Austria
Area: 646 sq. feet
Construction date: 1992
Photographs: Paul Ott

Floor plan

1. Access - 2. Corridor/Living room - 3. Bedroom

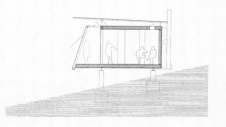

Section

The predominance of wood inside the building accentuates the lightness of the cabin. It also makes the place warm and welcoming. Unification of materials generates a greater spatial flexibility, a sense of depth.

Hornegg Complex

Hans Gangoly

The Hornegg complex in Preding (Austria) with three residences acquired its present appearance through successive interventions in the course of its history. The work of Daniel von Lapp in 1875 marked the first phase.

In spring of 1997 the attic of the main building was destroyed due to a fire. The incident was taken advantage of to create new spaces. The beautiful panoramic views provided 360 degree views of the town and the Hornegg Palace. The operation consisted of an additional volume that was both aesthetically and structurally light. For this reason, a prefabricated structure was chosen.

The system of columns and metallic beams are situated behind the façade. In contrast to the brick wall and few apertures of the existing house, the glass façade runs the entire perimeter of the new volume. The façades are sealed with aluminum sheets that envelop the glass surface and roll up on the upper floor.

The volume establishes a double height that is put to use in each home as an alternative space which allows access to the roof terraces.

The residences are spacious and diaphanous. Each one contains a living and dining room integrated with the kitchen, one bedroom and one bathroom. The alternative space is located on the upper section where the access to the terraces is situated.

In contrast to the cool aspect of the façade, the interiors feature a warm atmosphere: the wood floors and dominant presence of white create a intimate and inviting space.

Architect: **Hans Gangoly**
Location: **Preding, Austria**
Area: **6.888 sq. feet**
Construction date: **1998**
Photographs: **Paul Ott**

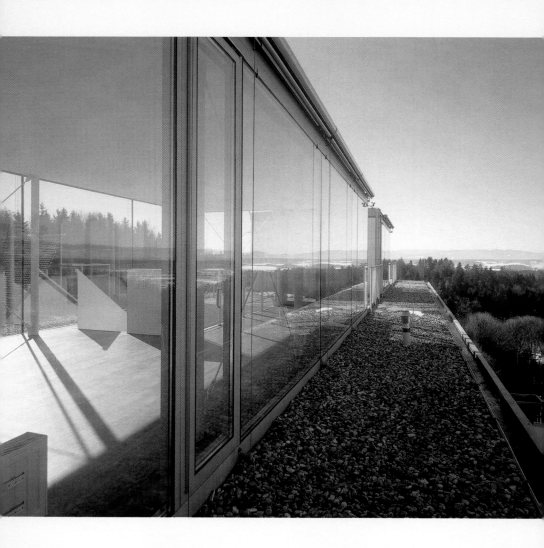

The upper bays are set back from the main block. They give the appearance of glass boxes set on top of the roof. The metal canopies used to close the upper parts offer greater security when desired, largely depending on the seasonal conditions.

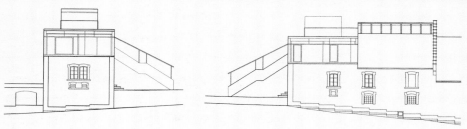

Sections

The regular rectangular shape and the building's perimetral structures made for the creation of well-defined spaces. These spaces, may, however, be redecorated for spatial variation. The relation between the different levels is brought out well by the predominance of the building's height, the staircase, and the great amount of natural light available.

1. Main access - 2. Living/dining room

3. Kitchen - 4. Bedroom - 5. Bathroom - 6. Den

7. Terrace

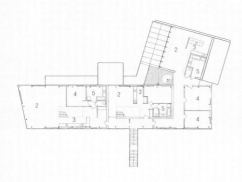
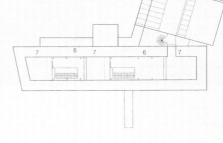

Ground floor   First floor

Multiresidential Buildings

Comtemporary architects are constantly evolving the concept of the home. and are also transforming the concept of social housing. They are re-establishing the often ill-perception of public residential buildings and transforming them into aesthetic. functional and economically viable living spaces. This section presents projects that include both private and social housing.

Leffe House

Studio Archea

Architects Laura Andreini, Marco Casamonti, and Giovanni Polazzi founded Studio Archea with the aim of creating "an architecture laboratory for experimental design." They consider each one of their activities an occasion to experiment with a wide range of forms and materials.

The single-family building raised in the Italian town of Leffe replaces a ruined construction in the historical center. It is a way of making way for a new program drawn up and distributed over different (again new) levels.

Among the particulars that conditioned the site location, the intention of respecting the alignment of the façade is a key factor. It was to adjust to the adjacent fronts, on the street level. Leffe House thus represents itself as a variation of the Gothic style that dominated the place. It is an interplay of planes that fold onto the convex part of the building like the porticos that open and break up the absolute flatness of the façade laid out on the urban elevation.

The dwelling is distributed over the five stories in a repetition of the irregular ground plan. This irregularity just goes right on up the construction, bringing about a succession of surprising interiors, deep perpendicular wells, double-height spaces, and a self-contained elevator shaft. The building's planned volume and the texture of its façades represent the rich design concept and the color scheme not only of the new architecture but of what surrounds it.

Architect: **Studio Archea**

Location: **Leffe. Bergamo. Italy**

Construction Date: **1998**

Photographs: **Pietro Savorelli, Alessandro Ciampi**

The Italian architects at Studio Archea planned
each of their activities as occasions to experiment
with a diversity of forms and materials.

In order to create a unique ambience, dissociated from that of the adjacent houses, the façade folds like an accordion. Practically closed and impenetrable, the surface is perforated by a series of long narrow windows that allow the entrance of natural light. The main street façade, slotted into the space between two buildings of different heights, opens onto the street. A system of shutters of stainless steel and rusted sheet copper close in a single plane that unifies the surface.

The façade --in the same phrasing of long, narrow apertures that look like big venetian blinds-- is in Santa Flora stone. The street façade folds back and forth in a metallic panel system which, at the same time, does not depart from the compositional unity that dominates the building's overall look.

The project, in the historical center of Leffe, near Bergamo, occupies a narrow strip-like site, characteristic of the parceling and urban distribution of this valley.

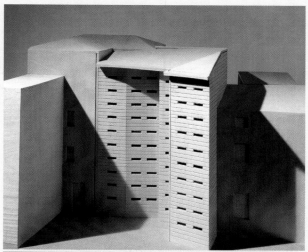

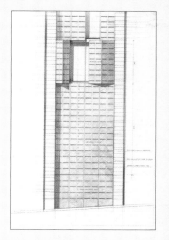

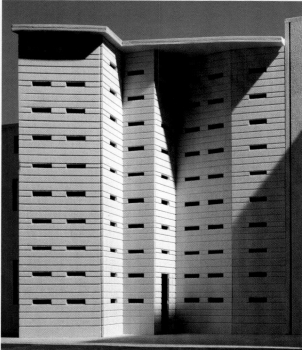

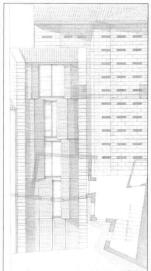

Sketch of elevations

The tower that contains the stairwell fits into the larger space between the complex space created by the peripheral façades of the building.

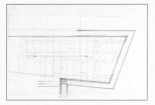

Detail of the stairwell

Distribution plans

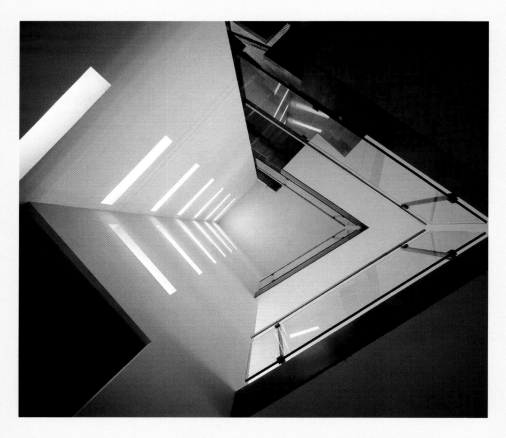

Tea Gardens Residence

Stephen Varady Architecture

The Tea Gardens residence is bordered on the south and west by a nature reserve; on the north, by a road; and on the east, by the only neighboring house. The building was carefully placed amid the existing vegetation, on top of a hillock, to take advantage of the views. A wall preserves the privacy of both homes.

From the outset, Stephen Varady envisioned the project as a sculpture. Conceptually, the work consists of a series of walls intersecting a prism on the ground. The north-south walls were painted blue and the east-west walls were painted gray. The layout of the house is sharply interrupted by a staircase that visually connects the part of the upper floor that faces north with the summer balcony, which faces south.

The design process was influenced by a deep awareness of the ecology, so these spaces are extremely energy-efficient. The windows, for example, are equipped with screens that strategically block the summer sun. The common areas enjoy excellent ventilation, and the roof can accommodate photovoltaic panels, which will be added when the system becomes more economically viable.

After thorough research, it was decided that the house would be built of concrete, for thermal inertia. Also, concrete is more economical than iron and wood, allowing for coverage of larger areas without significantly increasing the budget. Some of the floors are concrete painted black, and others were covered with strips of wood. The finishing is also wood.

Architect: Stephen Varady Architecture
Collaborator: Scott Hoy
Construction date: 2000
Location: Tea Gardens, New South Wales, Australia
Area: 3548 sq. feet
Photographs: Stephen Varady and Rusell Pell

One of the architects' goals was to plan a building that would age gracefully. They wanted the walls to be enhanced by age as the weather improved the patina.

Cross-section

0 1 2

The home is on two levels. The lower-ground floor houses the garage, the rainwater tank, and a storage room; the living quarters are on the upper floor.

1. Entry hall - 2. Bathroom - 3. Garage
4. Workshop - 5. Water tank - 6. Bedrooms
7. Bathroom - 8. Balconies - 9. Living room
10. Study - 11. Dining room - 12. Kitchen
13. Bathroom - 14. Master bedroom

Lower-ground floor

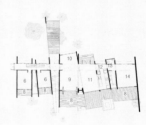

0 1 2

Upper floor

Residences in Haarlemmerbuurt

Felix Claus, Kees Haan

The Haarlemmerbuurt district is located between the Amsterdam port and the city's canals. The area is lively and is characterized by atmospheric mix of the bourgeois of the canals and the landscape of the Ij riverbank.

The history of this area in Amsterdam is reflected in the façades of the houses. Just as in a film, the homes constitute a string of architectural styles from all epochs sewn into each other.

In the case of the Binnenwieringerstraat, the act is realized upon an existing structure: a very small, 3.5 m wide by 8 m deep space. For this reason, the architects decided to allocate the service areas and installations in an adjacent space so that the original building could house a comfortable apartment. After its remodelling the existing structure only disposed of three bedrooms. This allowed the preservation of the previous structure and its typical hand-crafted constructive details (which would be impossible to reproduce today) during the instalment of installations, stairs, ventilation tubes... In short, everything that is necessary to adjust the project to the norms and contemporary customs was allocated to the annexe. The aged building, instead of becoming a museum of residences from the last century, is transformed into an open plan of 7 x 3 meters, which signifies a luxury in residential typology.

Architect: Felix Claus, Kees Haan

Collaborators: Floor Arons, Roland Rens, Michael van Pelt [design], Stracke [structure].

Location: Binnenwieringerstraat 8, Amsterdam, Holland.

Completion date: April 1995.

Promoter: Lieven de Key.

Program: Apartments.

Photographs: Ger van der Vlugt.

Residences in the historical center of Maastricht

Mecanoo

The objective of the architects in charge of this project in Maastricht was to restore the intimacy of a great square that in its time served as a central patio for businesses and small farms and which over time got lost amidst the chaos of the city. The residences are situated behind a varnished cedar screen that conceals the living rooms. The terraces and galleries through which the residences are accessed by way of common stairs are resolved in the same fashion as the perimetral portico—pavement with quartzite. The gallery connects the two blocks which compose the concept of the project, creating the illusion of a single façade which in reality is made up of two individual entities.

The interior distribution is reminiscent of traditional Dutch houses, each home occupying the totality of the space. One block is occupied by a duplex, from façade to façade and several residences that occupy the corner facing the square. The lateral façade of the latter, behind which the bedrooms are located, is painted in white to differentiate it from those finished in wood.

The interior patios consist of gardens belonging to the ground floor apartments and small storage cubicles made from a special regional stone that was salvaged from a nearby demolition. The stone is also implemented in the cladding of the nucleus stairs and in the reconstruction of the wall that defines and limits the site.

Architect: Mecanoo
Collaborator: ABT Technical Consultants, Delft.
Location: Herdenkingsplein "memory plaza".
Maastricht. Holland.
Project date: 1990●1992.
Construction date: 1994.
Client: City hall of Maastricht [plaza]. Stichting Pensioenfonds Rabobank [residences].
Program: 52 apartments.
Photographs: Christian Richter.

Residences on Calle del Carme o Calle d'En Roig

Josep Llinàs Carmona

In the historical center of Barcelona, the area of the Raval is suffering a series of transformations and operations upon a dense network of residential buildings that are gradually deteriorating.

The site, fruit of a demolition of various buildings, gives onto the narrow and dark street—calle d'En Roig—and the commercial and lively street—calle del Carme. The great length of the façade facing calle d'En Roig offered the possibility of bettering its quality. Diverse operations facilitated the improvement of the previous conditions, as much from the perspective of the residences as from the urban context in which they are found.

The ground floor opens in the shape of a funnel towards Carme street, allowing the passage of pedestrians. The first floor introduces three small towers that permit the widening of this section and the consequent entry of natural light from such a dark street. The first floor is the area which most adapts to its existing perimeter through the contour of the towers at the extremities and a curtain of moss that unites them, protecting the intimacy of the terraces that face the neighboring façade.

The three volumes are situated over a new broken façade line that originates from a discontinuous baseboard. The largest of the three, in the corner, resumes its original entrance through a 5 meter projection that advances the upper floors over its neighbors. The second is attached to the far limits of the site and the third recedes, remaining least visible from the street.

Architect: Josep Llinàs Carmona
Collaborators: Eva Monte. Joan Vera. Jaume Martí.
Client: Procivesa.
Location: Barcelona. España.
Project date: 1992–1993.
Construction date: 1994–1995.
Program: 28 residences, commercial spaces, and parking.
Photographs: David Cardelús.

Grand Union Walk

Nicholas Grimshaw ○ Partners Ltd

The principal objective of this commercial and residential complex is to reconcile architectural and high-tech possibilites with the necessities of urban planning posed by society today. The architects opted for the construction of a complex composed of large warehouses, a network of studios and a group of attached residences, all upon a triangular site. Consequently, the land enabled the segregation of the lot into units due to the differing direction of the laterals of the intervention area. The last two units were reserved for the commercial and office areas, while the nucleus of residences was allocated in the north wing to offer a suggestive combination of modern architecture and nature. The important role conceded to the physical presence of water in its relation to the building was to equally provide the security of future tenants and to protect the state of the canal. The use of characteristic convex structures for the façade searches to reduce the risks of obliqueness, reinforce the privacy of each of the terraces and increase the visibility over the canal.

The intervention based its proposals on essential points: the almost industrial process of structures' assembly, the alternating presence of straight,curved, transparent and opaque surfaces and a measured relationship between exterior and interior spaces.

Architect: Nicholas Grimshaw ○ Partners Ltd
Collaborators: Neven Sidor, Mark Fisher, Hin Tan. Ingrid Bille, Sally Draper, James Finestone, Thomas Fink, Rowena Fuller, Andrew Hall, Christine Humphrey, Gunther Schnell, Ulrike Seifritz, Simon Templeton.
Location: Grand Union Walk, Candem, London, United Kingdom.
Construction date: 1986○1989.
Client: J.Sainsbury, plc. Architects: Nicholas Grimshaw ○ Partners Ltd.
Program: Residential and commercial complex: shopping center, warehouses and residences.
Photographs: John Peck.

Apartment building in Basilea

Jacques Herzog, Pierre de Meuron

The project consists of a small building located in a site of the old medieval fabric of Basilea. It is narrow and long: 20 feet wide and 75 meters deep. The building occupies the entire parcel establishing a distribution of residences based on a very unusual depth, which is resolved with the inclusion of a patio. The distribution of the floors is conditioned by the existence of this large grassy patio situated in one of the neighboring buildings that faces south. In this manner, the residences dispose of views over the trees of the garden.

The entire structure is supported by two lateral brick walls, thicker than normal, that translate to the street façade where they emerge as thick party walls that clearly delineate the neighboring buildings.

The ground floor contains a double-height vestibule that allows access into an existing museum at the rear of the lot. The first two floors are designated to commercial spaces. The apartments' street façade closes off by way of molded iron shutters that occupy the width and height of every floor. The choice for this uncommon material relates to various elements of the urban furnishings, such as the street and sewage grilles. The building adopts an urban appearance based on characteristic street elements.

Architects: Jacques Herzog, Pierre de Meuron
Collaborators: Dieter Jüngling, Rina Plangger.
Project director: André Maeder.
Client: Pensionkasse des Basler Staatspersonals, BS.
Location: Schützenmattstrasse, Basilea,
Switzerland.
Project date: 1991.
Construction date: 1992-1993.
Photographs: Margherita Spiluttini.

Residential building in Oporto

Eduardo Souto de Moura

The Rua do Teatro is located in an area of Oporto, exterior to the medieval city walls. The new residential building is situated inside a plot that is much wider than the surrounding ones. Given that the neighboring residences are relatively small-scale, Souto de Moura proposes through this project a continuity of the language spoken by the surrounding architecture. The two adjacent structures possess different dimensions: the left is taller and deeper, and the right is lower and far more shallow. These circumstances led Souto de Moura to establish a volumetric plan that strictly respects the alignment of neighboring buildings so that the project itself would be in charge of assuming the change. In this way, the two resulting bodies, clearly differentiated, resume the smallest scale of the neighboring buildings.

Also, the last two floors of each building recede, transforming two blocks into four. The final decision of the deconstruction process consists of placing the stairwell on the axis between the two volumes, creating a fifth volume, somewhat taller, that concludes the composition.

The tall volume houses five floors and the lowest houses four. The distribution of the residences is simple. The first three floors dispose of two homes per landing and the last two floors contains two large duplexes accessed by a lift.

Architect: Eduardo Souto de Moura
Collaborators: Graça Correia. Pedro Mendes. Silvia Alves. Francisco Cunha. Manuela Lara.
Constructor: Soares da Costa / San José.
Client: Eng. Miguel Cerquinho.
Location: Rua do Teatro. Oporto. Portugal.
Project date: 1992.
Construction date: 1995.
Photographs: Luis Ferreira Alves.

Residential complex Kop van Zuid

Frits van Dongen

The complex, which houses 625 residences, is situated on a stretch of land that was previously a dock, three sides of which touch the river, two longer ones on each lateral side and a third at the other extremity.

The complex features an elongated jetty with a system of linear blocks that form three semi-closed patios. Tall transversal blocks, designated to massive housing, separate smaller blocks that house a string of single-family homes and which close off the stretches parallel to the jetty. This forms a scheme of five large and equally distanced blocks that are also different from each other.

Apart from these three patios, a large open intermediate space is destined to a public garden placed on top of the parking area.

The operations of alteration are practically guaranteed by the initial proposal. In this way, access corridors within the staggered blocks, situated on the dorsal spine, unite in height, two by two, forming a double space that results in an elevated access to the top residential floors. Halfway down the block a large, glass-fronted patio permits the maximum entry of light into the common zones of this central interior, in which the bathrooms and kitchens are located. The single family houses, orientated toward the lateral jetties, have a particular feature: here a meticulous study of the unity of the residence is resolved with regularity.

Architect: Frits van Dongen

Collaborators: A. J Mout, P. Puljiz, A. J. de Haas, M. Heesterbeek, F. Veerman, J. van Hettema, J. Molenaar.

Program: 625 residences, I sports club, 6 tennis courts, children's play area, 10,160 sq. feet of commercial spaces, and 200 parking spaces.

Location: Landtong, Rotterdam, Holland.

Construction date: 1998.

Photographs: Daria Scagliola ○ Stijn Brakkee.

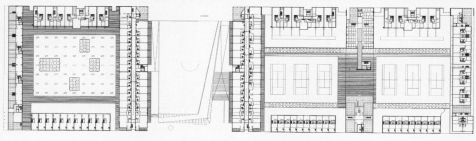

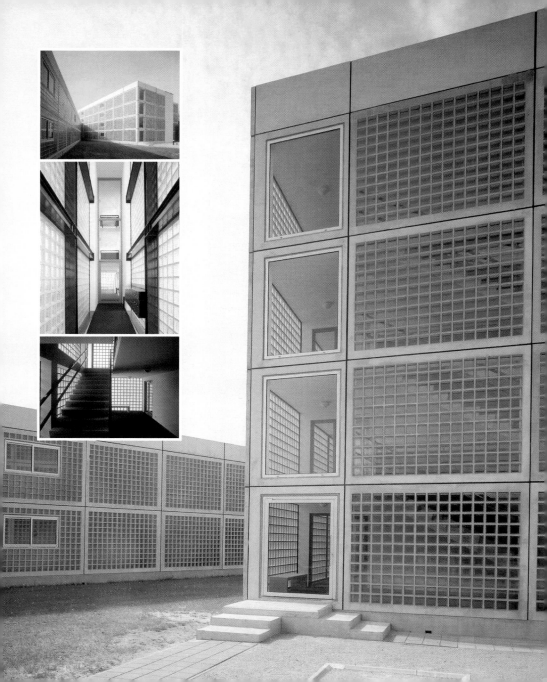

Apartments in Tilburg

Wiel Arets S.L.

This previously industrial area of the center of Tilburg is witnessing a transformation. The De Pond museum, for example, was installed inside one of the old factories of the area. The apartments proposed be Arets are distributed into three blocks on Timmermanspad street, the same street occupied by the museum. Two of them are positioned in a U-shape at one of the museum's extremities, creating an interior garden adjoining one of its façades, and the third is an elongated block with views over the De Pond garden just on the lot opposite its main entrance.

The success of the project is probably due to the overlapping of the apartment building and the museum as well as to the decision to adopt the same internal organization and treatment of the façade for all three buildings.

Each apartment has a 828 square foot surface area. A ten-foot wide common corridor provides access to each of them.

The exterior treatment of the buildings' façades vary depending on whether these are main façades that face the street or rear façades that protect the corridor that leads to the apartments. One is rough stucco, "putz" style, with interior balconies from where the street is visible. The other, always giving onto garden areas, incorporates glass block walls with large windows, illuminating the ten-foot wide corridor.

Architect: Wiel Arets S.L.
Client: Stichting Verenigde Woningcorporaties SVW.
Collaborators: Michel Melenhorts (coordinator).
Tina Brandt, Reina Bos, Andrea Wallrath; DVHV Amersfoort (budget).
Program: 67 three-bedroom apartments divided into three blocks of 37, 14 y 16 units.
Location: Timmermanspad Street, on the corner of Kuiperstraat, Tilburg, Holland.
Construction date: 1993-1995.
Photographs: Kim Zwarts.

Apartments in Graz

Ernst Giselbrecht

The building is situated on a north to south axis and is composed of four floors grouped by two, in the form of a duplex. Those that occupy the last two floors enjoy a balcony and views of the area, while those on the ground floor have direct access to the garden. The accesses, stairs and balconies are not distributed symmetrically, Rather, they appear as independent elements that vary formally depending on their use or function.The walls that divide the apartments run through the entire building and establish the dominant rhythm of the interior structure. Each pair of residences is united by a gallery. The scheme of walls and apertures allows the liberal subdivision of the apartments, forming a structural system determined by a spirit of classic modernism. Thanks to the generous amount of glass used in the building, the entire volume can be perceived from the main entrance.

The stairwell appears as a continuous element that runs through the building until it reaches the roof. The transparence of the upper floors and its internal divisions transforms the different bedrooms into independent bodies within a common space. In this way, the perception of the place results visually amplified, provoking a global visualization of the apartment and the opaque walls that dilute in the great multifunctional space that constitutes the complex.

Architect: **Ernst Giselbrecht.**
Location: **Graz, Austria.**
Construction date: **1998.**
Photographs: **Paul Ott.**

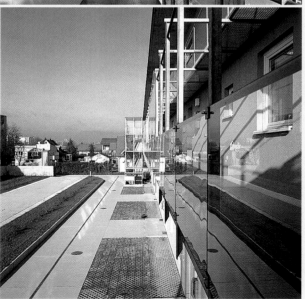

Residential complex La Venerie

Dubosc ○ Landowski

In this residential complex, two symmetrical blocks confront each other creating an interior space that is more controlled, protected and integrated into the urban framework of Montargis. The architects Dubosc and Landowski intend to change the pessimistic tone associated with social housing and propose an alternative in which the spacial quality, the materials and the relationship with the exterior distance themselves from general public projects.

The project makes the most of the useful surface area offered by a constructed space. This is accomplished through the positioning of the staircases outside of the building, thus reducing the collective zones which rarely receive any activity.

The residences are distributed transversally to the blocks, which allow them to possess a double orientation. On the ground floor the distribution is vertical. These residences are duplexes designated for four or five people with direct access to a private garden. The second level is formed by units designated for one or two persons, and are orientated longitudinally and accessed by exterior corridors and stairs. The last two floors are occupied by residences for two to three persons organized once again as duplexes.

The materials employed are of industrial origin, which permits an uncomplicated assemblage process and minimal maintenance.

The residential complex of LaVenerie is a new architectural proposal that intends to reconcile the social dimensions of collective housing and the inherent autonomy of individual homes.

Architect: Dubosc ○ Landowski
Collaborators: Andrea Mueller, Monica Alexandrescu.
Program: 48 residences.
Client: OPAC du Loiret.
Location: Montargis, Loiret, France.
Construction date: 1994.
Photographs: J. M. Monthiers.

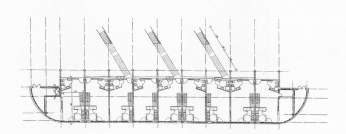

Residential complex in Graz

Riegler ○ Riewe

This residential complex is situated on the south periphery of the Austrian city of Graz, in an area of the city that gradually extends towards rural zones. The building intends to reflect this transitional situation.

There are two types of dwellings in the building: ones that are 50 m2 which contain two and a half rooms and others that measure 78 m2 with four and a half rooms. The two distribution possibilites lend these living spaces great flexibility and use.

The volume, three floors high and 75 meters in length, aims towards an unconventional appearance through its exterior skin. Sliding doors run across the totality of the length of the façades. The façade with access to the dwelllings is interrupted by the openings for the stairs. Metallic mesh was used as the cladding material for this façade, rigid on the staircases and mobile on the homes. In contrast, nylon was used for the façade that looks onto the garden. A continual movement of the protective doors, which shield from the sun and provide intimacy, offer constantly varying images, juxtaposed within the successive openings.

The most urban façade, close to a street, features rugs over hard pavement that mark the entrance to the doors in the way of a ramp-stairway.

On the other side, a garden grants a more direct contact with the exterior on the side through which each home disposes of the greatest length of façade and where the living rooms are located.

Architect: Riegler ○ Riewe
Collaborators: Margarethe Müller, Brigitte Theissl.
Program: 27 viviendas.
Location: Banhofstraße, Graz, Austria.
Project date: 1991.
Construction date: 1994.
Photographs: Margherita Spiluttini, Paul Ott.

Building 113 on Oberkampf Street

Frederic Borel

The context of the project is an urban site that measures 20 meters in width and 87 meters in length. Along with these awkward dimensions, another difficulty was the presence of common median walls with a maximum height of 23 meters.

Contained within natural limits, similar to fortress walls, the project transforms into a microterritory, an urban microcosmos.

The specific requisites of the program, which consist of a post-office and the construction of small apartments and studios for young people, became the active parameters of the project.

The post-office, stores and entrance to the residences are organized around a transparency through which we perceive a small fraction of the infinite: "presence and absence at a distance."

A small landscape, a garden visible from the street, is inserted into the space designated to distribution. The residences occupy the periphery of the site and possess views of the garden: the fragment of earth that breathes and the last façade which looks towards the sky.

The final area at the deepest part of the parcel contains three levels of living space with terraces orientated towards the south. The configuration of the apartments, designed for young couples, proposes a space adaptable to the evolution of a family. The center of the domestic space can be used as a children's room, master bedroom, a library-studio or just as well house the living room.

Architect: Frederic Borel

Location: Building 113, Rue Oberkampf, Paris, France.

Construction date: November, 1993.

Client: Department of Telecomunications and Postal Service.

Collaborators: Joel Gallouedec, Carola Brammen, Massimo Mattiussi, SCGPM [contractor], G.I.I. [Engineer].

Program: 80 apartments, building for a post office and a small shopping mall.

Area: 15, 320 sq. feet

Photographs: F. Borel.

Housing for Post Service employees

Philippe Gazeau

The site on which the 26 residences are located is extremely narrow and long, situated in a heterogenous environment from which the regular and urban façade stands out among the presence of lower and more irregular volumes situated at the rear. The project's aims were to resolve the difficult entry of light and ventilation into the intermediate zone of the site, adapting to the volumes and establishing a harmonious relationship with the surrounding structures.

On the side of Rue de l'Ourcq, three tall volumes (ground floor + 7) rest against the two lateral party walls and recede a considerable distance in relation to the alignment with the street. The last two floors recedes progressively further, such that the height perceived from the street is less (ground floor + 5). The appearance of the two entities of unequal width, separated by a large void is a determining factor in its perception from the street.

The central void between the two buildings creates a large corridor on the ground level which runs longitudinally through the site until the end, where a small communal garden allows the recession of the rear façade. This central gap, quite wide in proportion to the residential spaces, contains all the vertical accesses. The spacious landings project a corner between the two blocks, creating an ample balcony.

Architect: Philippe Gazeau
Collaborators: Agnès Cantin, Jacques Forte.
Constructor: Fougerolle Construction.
Client: SA HLM Toit et Joie.
Program: 26 residences for Postal Service employees.
Location: 46, Rue de l'Ourcq, Paris, France.
Construction date: 1993.
Photographs: Jean Marie Monthiers.

Les Chartrons Residence

François Marzelle, Isabelle Manescau, Edouard Steeg

The Les Chartrons residence is located in the center of the city and constitues an experiment to achieve quantitative, functional and aesthetic parameters which correspond to a quality of life acceptable to these kinds of residences. The concept begins with the idea that all the main bedrooms should include an en-suite bathroom, constituting a basic model whose repetition and variation is to organize the entire complex. This module, repeated five times, forms part of a major unit composed of five bedrooms that share a comon living room and kitchen. The distribution is simple: the lower floor contains two bedrooms and common areas, while the upper floor houses the remaining three bedrooms. An interior stairwell communicates the two floors, imparting a certain conventional character to the unit. Nevertheless, each of the five rooms can be accessed independently, affording the sytem of stairs a relevant complexity and importance.

The project is organized around two parallel four-floor blocks that create a somewhat narrow interior patio. All the systems of stairwells originate from this patio, leading to the apartments. The appearance of the patio is afforded by the presence of wooden shutters that close off the galleries of the façade.

Architect: François Marzelle, Isabelle Manescau, Edouard Steeg.
Client: Sonacotra.
Program: Residence with 102 rooms.
Location: Rue Poyenne, Burdeos, France.
Project date: 1991.
Construction date: 1994.
Photographs: Vicent Monthiers Schlomoff.

Wozocos

MVRDV

The team of Dutch architects known as MVRDV received the assignment of realizing a block of 100 apartments for elderly people in an area west of the center of Amsterdam. After analyzing the urbanistic norms written by Van Eesteren for the given area, they reach the conclusion that only 87 of the 100 aparments could be accomplished without blocking the entry of sunlight into the neighboring buildings. Where could the remaining 13 be placed? Architects decided to hang them on the north façade by suspending in mid-air, literally.

In the building, a corridor on the north façade, accessed solely by a nucleus of stairs and a lift, provides access to the each of the apartments, both those inside and those that project outwards. The apartments also give onto the south façade. These consist of three dwellings that revolve around a perimetral living area in which reside the kitchen, living-dining room and a bedroom with a balcony. The balconies vary in size and the color of the material in which they are finished, as do the windows, whose distribution appear to be independent in respect to the composition of the floors, some of them coinciding with the dividing wall between residences.

The projectiles are constructed with a metallic framework, reinforced by diagonals that anchor to the divisory walls between the units of each structure. The walls are wider than strictly necessary to better the acoustic insulation of the residences.

Architect: MVRDV

Collaborators: Willem Timmer, Arjan Mulder, Frans de Witte, Bureau Bouwkunde.

Structure: Pieters Bouw Techniek, Haarlem.

Client: Woningbouwvereniging Het Oosten.

Program: 100 residences for elderly people in the west district of Amsterdam.

Location: Woonzorgcomplex Joh. De Deo. Reimerswaalstraat, Amsterdam=Osdorp, Holland.

Construction date: 1994=1997.

Photographs: Hans Werlemann.

Social housing in Alcobendas

Manuel de las Casas

This project encompasses 198 officially protected dwellings. The complex is formed by a series of rectangular volumes perpendicular to the traffic, and others parallel to the extremes of the lot which visually enclose the complex. The residential blocks are deformed by the sides correspondent to the street, creating a façade and closing off the interior spaces from the noise and views of the traffic.

The complex is a residential unit, that is, the lot is sectioned so that the spaces in between the blocks are private and pedestrian.

The five-floor volumes incorporate a high density of living spaces: four per floor. The dwellings are established in a linear form. The service and storage areas are allocated in the central nucleus of which most give onto two façades for better ventilation.

The structure and boundaries with the exterior are resolved by a system of large, 4.6inch thick reinforced concrete panels that act as structural walls and are forged by 2.7inch thick concrete tiles.

These panels are used for the façade, just as they are for the interior and for the transversal walls, yielding great rigidity to the complex. The general use of prefabricated elements also permitted an important reduction of the time needed to complete project and precision in the final finishes that are difficult to attain through conventional systems of construction.

Architect: Manuel de las Casas

Collaborators: José Luis Cano, Indagsa (constructors), Ortiz ○ Cia (installations), Felicidad Rodríguez (plastic), Iciar de las Casas (garden and landscape).

Constructor: Ortiz ○ Cia.

Client: Ivima.

Program: 198 social residences and garages, 183 three○bedroom apartments (753 sq. feet), 15two○bedroom apartments (645 sq. feet), 84 parking spaces.

Location: Alcobendas, Madrid, Spain.

Project date: 1993.

Construction date: 1996.

Photographs: Ángel Luis Baltanás, Eduardo Sánchez.

Apartments

Apartments come in a variety of shapes and sizes. This chapter runs through a selection of the most popular today: small studios, the apartment and office, and loft spaces, all designed by the best of contemporary architects and packed with ideas on how to make the most of a living space.

Apartment in Stockholm

Claesson Koivisto Rune Arkitektkontor

This private apartment was commissioned by a young businessman who wanted a serene haven from work where he could disconnect and relax. Originally a typical late nineteenth-century Stockholm apartment with wood floors, panelling, and a tiled stove, it was decided that half of the space—the living room—would be maintained, and the other half—the kitchen, bathroom, and bedroom—would be completely redone in a modern style. To emphasize the contrast, the modern area was painted in a light gray, and the original part was kept white. The plan was to create a flowing visual cross communication between elements. From the entrance hallway, a curved corner leads to the first axis that contains the bathroom, kitchen, and bedroom. The intersecting axis runs along the kitchen into the living room where a wall-mounted shelf is at the exact same height as the kitchen counter. A series of vertical and horizontal glass panels divide the sections: Between the entrance area and the bathroom is a vertical dimmed glass door; between the kitchen and bathroom a horizontal acid-etched glass window; between the living room and bedroom a vertical transparent glass panel; and sunk into the far wall of the bedroom, a horizontal acid-etched mirror glass that creates an illusion of continuous space. The furniture, mostly designed by the architects, displays pure lines and curves throughout the space, minimalist yet never cold or uncomfortable. It is an example of impeccable and functional design that whispers a sense of calm.

Architect: Claesson Koivisto Rune Arkitektkontor
Location: Stockholm, Sweden
Completion Date: 1999
Surface Area: 645 square feet
Photographs: Patrik Engquist

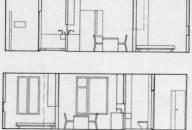

There is a noticeable emphasis placed on horizontal lines, expressed through long niches along bare surfaces and the series of cupboards across the living room wall. These lines give the illusion of extended space.

The glass window between the bathroom and kitchen lights up in one room when the light is turned on in the other.

Bathtub and basin in cedar-wood are custom-designed by the architects.

Flat in Barcelona

Eva Prats y Ricardo Flores

This young couple's flat occupies the former attic of an single-family house located in Sarrià, an area of central Barcelona. The space was thought out as open plan; the only enclosed area is the bathroom unit, around which all other household activities revolve. Distributed on two floors, the lower level consists of the bathroom facing the front door, which opens out into a reception hall, kitchen/dining, and living area. All first floor spaces look out on a private garden terrace through full-height, wall-to-wall glass doors. A tall storage unit in the kitchen partly secludes this area, while the dining table beside leads the way to a comfortable lounge area that incorporates a corner sofa. The bedroom, directly above the bathroom, is accessible by way of a staircase that climbs up a wall next to the entrance. The neutral palette is created mainly by dark wood on floors and furniture and pure white on walls, accentuated by a few colored pieces. Wall niches and shelves hold books and ornaments. Light fixtures hang low from the ceiling or stand upright on the floor, while the height at which the apartment is situated allows for natural light to filter through at different points throughout the space.

Architect: Eva Prats and Ricardo Flores
Location: Barcelona, Spain
Year of Completion: 1997
Area: 965 square feet
Photographs: Eugeni Pons

A folding dining table opens out to accommodate dinner guests.

Here, the bathroom was selected as the only room in the house to be enclosed, making the surrounding areas more spacious and luminous.

The kitchen cabinet serves as a pantry while also forming a visual barrier between the living and eating areas. The side that faces the living room is painted white, making it look like a small partition.

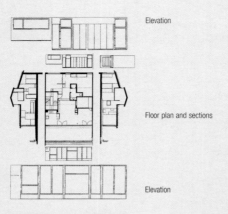

Elevation

Floor plan and sections

Elevation

The four sections surrounding the bathroom floor
plan illustrate the different functions of each area.

Hollywood Hills

Finn Kappe

"Making the most with the least is the practice of alchemists and architects." Based on this philosophy, Finn Kappe has created this small living space located in the backyard of a 1940s Hollywood Hills house. The poolhouse finds itself surrounded by a lush garden; a long rectangular space that consists of a single living area with a kitchen and bathroom. Set against a concrete wall, the lateral and front sides are purely transparent. Fleetwood sliding glass doors surround the space, admitting uninterrupted views of the garden. The narrowness of the space is disguised by this feature that gives the sensation of expanse. The glass doors open out to a narrow porch, over which stretches a slatted wood panel that runs the length of the house, shielding it from sun and heat. The interiors, inspired by mid-century modern residences, appears very contemporary. Large stone tiles, a concrete fireplace, a tatami bed, a small kitchen, and modern shower are slotted into this single area, with plenty of space left over. The bed and low stool are placed in the center against the wall facing the garden. The concrete block that contains the fireplace extends towards the wall and arranges the niches that serve as shelves.

The kitchen is integrated into this area, and just behind lies the shower room, which can be closed off by a door. The project is an interesting composition of linear forms and simple materials that defy common notions concerning small spaces.

Architect: Finn Kappe
Location: California, US
Completion Date: 2000
Surface Area: 380 square feet
Photographs: Michael Weschler

View from the adjacent garden: A continuous slatted panel shadowes the glass-fronted living spaces.

An unusual entrance with a sliding door adds visual interest, in this case revealing views of the greenery beyond.

New York Extension

Hanrahan o Meyers Architects

This project consists of an addition to an existing larger house that was also completely renovated including the floors, cabinetry, panelling, windows, stairs, and furnishings. Linking the original house with the new addition is a copper wall that wraps from a connecting hall to the facade of the existing house, where a new window in the living room completes the composition. The addition has cedar siding finished with a warm natural wood. Its major feature however is a blue wall that runs the length of the building and acts as a "new horizon" line, reestablishing the horizon within the house. It is also a reference to Luis Barragan's blue wall at Las Arboledas in Mexico City. The way in which the blue paint was laid gives the wall a velvety effect, adding a warm and inviting texture to the bedroom. The bed is made of wood a few shades darker than the surrounding wood, creating a contrast against the tall structure behind it that houses a closet and dresser. This structure stops short of the ceiling to permit the flow of light and to enhance the sense of continuous space. Beyond this room, a bathroom finished in stone has views to the surrounding garden. A frontal view of the addition displays a wonderful interaction between the blue "horizon" and the great blue pool that sits quietly out on the deck in front. The small pavillion that contains the addition can be used as an extra room or even as a guest house enjoying spectacular views of the pool and flourishing garden.

Architect: Hanrahan o Meyers Architects
Location: New York, US
Completion Date: 2001
Area: 1,200 square feet
Photographs: Peter Aaron [Esto]

Avoid interference by situating staircases against walls. Slatted steps permit the flow of light and enhance the sense of space.

The bedroom features a closet contained within a freestanding box that acts as a headboard for the bed.

View of the addition and existing house: The windows create a visual composition that adds interest to the structure's facade.

View from the existing house: A long hallway that leads to the new annex.

The extension is enveloped in tall windows that afford generous views of the outside garden.

A raised deck that extends outwards is imitated by the roof, which protects the space from the sun and heat.

Outskirts of Barcelona

GCA Architects

This apartment with approximately 750 square feet of floor space is located on the lower floor of a two-story house, and belongs to one of the sons of the couple that lives upstairs. The arrangement and distribution of the space is thought out to fit the needs of a single person. The various areas share a fairly open and continuous space, divided by sliding doors and the arrangement of furniture. On either side of the kitchen lie the living areas. The living room is comprised of an unenclosed area with a couple of armchairs and a sofa in white, a narrow center table, and shelves along the wall for ornaments. On the other side is the bedroom, which can be closed off by sliding matte glass doors. Around a corner and beyond the bedroom is a small wardrobe and bathroom. A large wooden panel behind the bed incorporates a long niche-shelf with warm spotlights placed along the inside. The kitchen displays stainless steel and blue-celeste cupboards that match the furniture and ceiling. The bathroom counter is made of iroko wood and the palette of the apartment is made up of blues, creams, and rich mochas.

Architect: GCA, Architects
Location: Barcelona, Spain
Completion Date: 2000
Area: 750 square feet
Photographs: Jose Luis Hausmann

The Smeg kitchen is integrated with the refrigerator and dishwasher. The island serves as a work table on one side and a dining table on the other. The vaulted ceiling has been painted to match the color scheme provided by the dining chairs from Habitat.

Sturdy wood shelves are both decorative and functional. Above them, spotlights face the ceiling to reflect a softer, more diffused light.

View of the bedroom and living room from the rear, where the bathroom is located. The bathroom counter is finished in iroko wood and the washbasin is stainless steel. The faucet is a design by Tara de Born Bracht and accessories are from Habitat.

Keep it simple: Small details are important even in a small living space. However, less is more if an uncluttered space is desired.

Loft in Barcelona

Nacho Marta

After tearing down walls and eliminating doors, this space—with some decorative inspiration—became a cozy one-bedroom apartment for a young single woman. The grand arch and pillars original to the previous living room have been preserved as a visual partition between the bedroom and lounge area. The only door that remains closes off the kitchen, while in the bedroom, a new large sliding door encloses a wardrobe and bathroom. The toilet lies behind another sliding door, leaving the closet and basin more accessible and open to view if desired. The space is distributed so that the wash-up area is not in direct view of any visitors in the living room, but easily reached without stumbling onto the privacy of the sleeping area, since the bed is placed at the other end in a corner. The tatami platform incorporates an extra surface for pillows and candles, acting as a second lounge, a reading spot, or as a night table. White, gray, and violets make up the color scheme, and a mix of curved and straight lines constitute the form of furniture and objects. A transparent inflatable armchair offers a place to sit but seems to take up virtually no physical space. In the tile bathroom, portable shelves provide extra space for toiletries. The solutions offered by this open plan space respond to concerns about lack of privacy, unifying the private and the public without losing the feeling of intimacy.

Architect: Nacho Marta
Stylist: Jorge Rangel
Location: Barcelona, Spain
Completion Date: 2000
Area: 805 square feet
Photographs: Jose Luis Hausmann

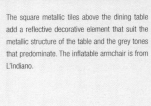

The square metallic tiles above the dining table add a reflective decorative element that suit the metallic structure of the table and the grey tones that predominate. The inflatable armchair is from L'Indiano.

A formal relationship between decorative elements makes a space cohesive and visually attractive.

A play between curved and straight lines is present in the composition of the space. The living room table features a pocket in which to keep extra magazines and books out of sight.

The bed rests on one side of the tatami platform, leaving an extra surface for personal space. The furry white bedcover was bought by the meter and the pillows are from DOM.

Barcelona House

Maximiá Torruella

Like many old and unrestored houses in Barcelona, this small apartment was based around a central corridor that led to several small rooms that received little or no natural light. As in most cases, the best solution was to remove all existing partitions and start from scratch. By opening up the area of the facade, the architects took advantage of the opportunity to enlarge the living room windows, creating an ample horizontal window and another smaller vertical one. This primary light source feeds light into the rest of the house, down the corridor, and all the way to the front door. The living room and dining area share a continuous floor space on either side of the hallway. A distinct feature is the relationship established between the dining room and kitchen by means of a communicating window in the kitchen wall that faces the dining table, through which conversations can take place, plates can be passed, and drinks can be served. The kitchen itself is an uncovered volume whose walls do not reach the ceiling, allowing the space to and also physically breathe aesthetically. Its sliding door allows it to remain open without blocking the way or taking up visual space. The palette consists of neutrals, greens, and yellows, and the furniture was designed by the architect and made to measure, keeping the space clean and uncluttered.

Architect: Maximiá Torruella
Location: Barcelona, Spain
Completion Date: 2000
Area: 828 square feet
Photographs: Jose Luis Hausmann

An antique bureau makes for a mini office space next to an entrance hall, concealed by a single partition.

The closets include a multitude of shelves, as well
as a mechanism that folds out to hang trousers or
to dry clothes.

Duplex in New York

John Butterworth

This small duplex was created by combining two apartments situated on different floors. The design revolved around the insertion of a new stair to connect the two levels, and integrating the spaces without taking away any area from the living quarters. An open staircase made of natural walnut was erected against the wall, linking top and bottom in a continuous path. The bottom floor is open plan, shared by the living room, dining room, and kitchen, differentiated only by the lowered ceiling in the kitchen area. On the level above, the stair is integrated within the walls of the private sleeping areas. A bedroom window filters light into the lower area. Throughout the space shelves are placed wherever possible, even high up under the ceilings to accommodate a privileged surface on which to place photographs and paintings. Materials were kept to a minimum, with white walls and ceilings providing a neutral background for other installations. Ebonized oak lines the floors, and a custom stainless steel kitchen and stair railing are lightweight constructions that accent rather than dominate the space. The bathrooms were renovated using a combination of mirror, porcelain, and glass to enhance the sense of lightness and space within a limited area. A framework of horizontal and vertical supporting structures give a perception of scale to the sparse elements of the living room, also accentuating the vertical movement that unifies the two spaces into one continuous and unified whole.

Architect: John Butterworth
Location: New York, US
Completion Date: 2001
Area: 690 square feet
Photographs: Paul Warchol

Duplex in Barcelona

Marisa Garcia y Alex Baeza

This duplex was rearranged to achieve a maximum use of available space with the help of specific colors, functional furniture, and careful illumination. First off, the TV room was lowered to the ground floor, leaving plenty of open space upstairs in which to arrange the living area that interacts with the terrace. The lower level also consists of the kitchen, office, bathrooms, guestroom, and master bedroom. The kitchen is composed of light wood cupboards and large white tiles. A long, narrow table in a corner designed as an office also doubles as a breakfast table. In the bathroom, the linearity offered by the minimalist furniture and accessories is contrasted by two sinuous and intertwining lamps suspended from a lilac ceiling. The staircase that leads upstairs is a steel structure coated in white and designed by Alex Baeza, while the wood steps and steel cables that support the structure are original to the space. This upper level consists of an open living area where certain furniture pieces of distinction stand out: the chaise longue by Le Corbusier, the original iron chair designed by Alex Baeza, and the standing sculpture by artist Pilar Massip. Along one side, a protruding suface was turned into a sofa by placing red cushions on top, leaving a space on one side for an office desk, and on the other for the stereo and speakers. Splashes of bright color, especially red, bring together the various styles and solutions afforded by this small, exemplary duplex.

Architects: Marisa Garcia and Alex Baeza
Location: Barcelona, Spain
Completion Date: 1999
Area: 860 square feet
Photographs: Jose Luis Hausmann

The dining table is made of sisú wood from the Mumbai Company. The chairs, chosen to contrast the table, are Pedrera models designed by Barba Corsini.

Two separate wheeled modules offer a surface for the TV and stereo, allowing great flexibility in their placement.

Curved and straight lines coexist to create a harmony of form.

Unusual lights and lamps offer a decorative solution for illuminating a home.

Rehabilitation in Barcelona

Anna Profitós, Deu i Deu

A redistribution of space meant tearing down several partitions and useless walls in this conventional-turned-stylish residential space. A restricted budget and imaginative coordination provided a challenge for the architects remodelling this home. After the structural changes were made, a certain amount of space was allocated to each area. In this case, the living room, dining room, and kitchen occupy most of the surface area, which is more or less square. A specific color combination of red, black, and white was chosen to decorate the living room. The series of shelves above the dark dining table create a decorative linear composition across the wall. A wall-mounted magazine and book holder leaves the wengué wood sufaces clear of clutter. Just before the kitchen, separated by way of a sliding glass door, are a counter and stools that serve as a breakfast area. The bedroom is also finished in black and white, Asian in style, with a matching matte black bed structure over tatami paper set into the floor. A graceful white orchid plant set against the black wall looking out on to the terrace makes the finishing touch. As for the bathrooms, one was designed "masculine", using neutral colors, stone, and wood, and the other "feminine," with more circular themes like the jewel-like colored stones applied to the blue wall. An imaginative approach to colors and styles along with resourceful thinking about space made this conventional home into a unique and most charming household.

Architect: Anna Profitós, Deu i Deu
Location: Barcelona, Spain
Completion Date: 2000
Area: 965 square feet
Photographs: Jose Luis Hausmann

A terrace view is opened up through the bedroom, offering a relaxing view of exterior plants and trees.

A series of spotlights illuminate paintings on the wall and books along shelves. A corner sofa offers a place to nap.

Shelf arrangements need not be conventional. An abstract system of shelves is a decorative element as well as a practical one.

The bedroom is composed of neutral colors that reflect the natural light from the terrace.

Residence in Bogotá

Guillermo Arias

This apartment occupies a large part of what was once a traditional residence in a building dating to the 1930s in Bogotá. The starting point for the project was the building's location: close to the congestion of the city center but on a tranquil and tree-lined street. The architects rebuilt the original exterior balcony facing the tree-lined street that had been torn down in previous renovations. The slope of one of the roofs was also altered, generating a longitudinal window for the entire upper part of the apartment that illuminates the back part of the space.

Finally, the architects moved the ceiling back in one of the rooms to create an interior patio that leads to the bedroom and isolates it from the immediate neighbors. Next to the entrance are a sink and a toilet on an elevated platform hidden behind a curved wall that leads to the main space. Once in this large room, various architectural elements differentiate each zone and give it character. The original chimney was pulled away from the lateral walls and opened on both sides. It now conjoins, dividing the kitchen from the living room. An axis of rectangular columns is detached from the foyer and demarcates the space for a large bookshelf that is elevated from the floor. The design of the woodwork emphasizes the horizontal lines and helps to blend the different zones. The furnishings and the lamps, designed by the architect, unify the formal language of the residence.

Architect: **Guillermo Arias**
Location: **Bogotá, Colombia**
Completion Date: **2000**
Area: **1,390 square feet**
Photographs: **Luis Cuartas**

A combination of shapes: Bathroom sinks do not
have to match. Here a square and a round washbasin produce an unusual pair.

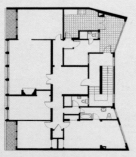

Previous floor-plan

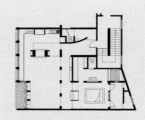

Actual floor-plan

A play of lines: Pillars and wall shelves create a criss-crossing pattern of vertical and horizontal lines.

A stainless steel kitchen and wall mounted oven and dishwasher are paired up with wood counters and shelves that offer both closed and open storage for utilities.

A large window framed in wood incorporates a shelf that serves as a night table behind the floor level bed.

The partition between kitchen and living room is more than just a divider: A fireplace for the living room and a spice rack for the kitchen.

Apartment in Bogotá

Luis Cuartas

This particular project occupies part of a building that previously contained the zones of the kitchen, the bathroom, and the dining room. After demolishing the existing walls, the architects envisioned the location of the new pieces that make up the residence. The goal was to create a continuous space with diverse relationships between the different areas, and a circular, unbroken path through the entire residence. After crossing the access, the circulation offers two alternatives. On the left side, a table extends all the way to the access and invites entry into the kitchen. On the right side, a corridor containing a large bench and a bath integrated with the chimney leads to the living room, which surprises with its double height. From here, a steel staircase leads to a walkway on the upper part where there is a small studio linked to a terrace. After having crossed the bedroom and the closet, the path ends, arriving once again at the kitchen. An elevated platform under the zone of the kitchen and bathroom conceals the installations and enriches the relationship between one space and another. The materials define the character of each zone of the residence. In the area close to the entrance, the smooth, painted cement floor continues until it is replaced by a wood dais in the more intimate area. The steel and glass structure of the walkway creates an aspect of lightness, while the walls that make up the interior volumes give a sensation of solidity.

Architect: Luis Cuartas
Location: Bogotá, Colombia
Completion Date: 2000
Area: 968 square feet
Photographs: Eduardo Consuegra

Narrow horizontal windows are accompanied by a skylight that filters light into the space. Mats and pillows turn an ordinary shelf into a sitting area.

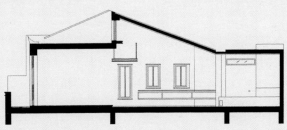

The combination of polished and unpolished surfaces enriches the texture and character of a space.

Previous floor plan

Actual floor plan

The kitchen space is fully utilized from floor to ceiling with shelves, cupboards, wall-mounted hooks, and integrated installations.

Space for Two

Guillermo Arias

This small, recreational apartment designed for a couple occupies what were once the two living rooms of an old residence in a 1930s building in Cartagena de Indias. Despite the apartment's splendid views of the Plaza Santo Domingo and the church, the interior was run-down, divided, and defined by a confusing and disorganized series of exposed beams. The first step was to reproduce the atmosphere that most likely existed in the original space, but in a contemporary language. A series of moldings with generous proportions define the general space, which is now continuous and free of dividing walls. Just after the entrance is a space that contains the zones of the kitchen, dining room, and living room. The kitchen is designed as an isolated table that contains all the appliances and functions as the dining room table. A low wall, with an incorporated bookshelf, relates this space to the bedroom. A sliding door made with strips of wood and interfacing also makes it possible to divide the areas. The headboard of the bed separates the bathroom from the bedroom and also functions as a closet. Almost all the details of the furnishings are incorporated into the interior architecture. The architect, Guillermo Arias, designed most of them himself: shelves, marble counter top in the bathroom, and kitchen cabinets, as well as all of the lamps. Arias is well known for his attention to detail. These gestures enrich this small space and give it formal unity.

Architect: **Guillermo Arias**
Location: **Cartagena de Indias, Colombia**
Completion Date: **1997**
Area: **860 square feet**
Photographs: **Carlos Tobón**

Kitchen objects can also be decorative: Wall niches are an alternative to ordinary shelves or cabinets.

An arched door frames the view of the church in the Plaza Santo Domingo. In the living room, a double-surface table offers a pocket for books and magazines.

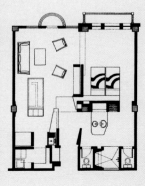

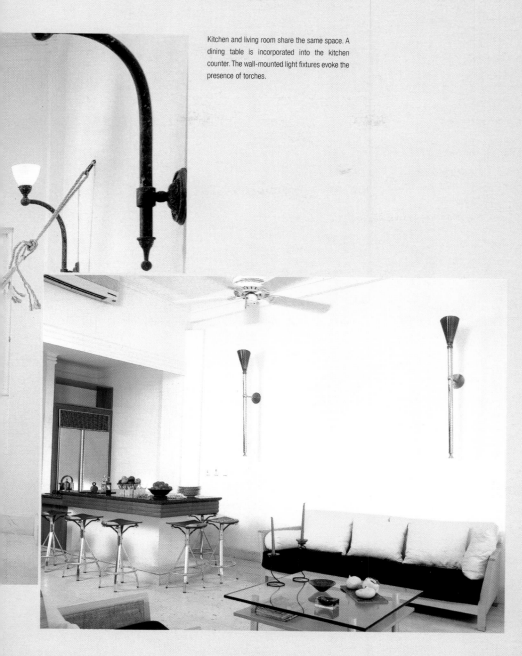

Kitchen and living room share the same space. A dining table is incorporated into the kitchen counter. The wall-mounted light fixtures evoke the presence of torches.

This seaside apartment displays a very urban chic style within a relatively small space, using lighting and storage techniques that keep it clean and unclutterred. At the entrance, a short corridor leads to a small room on the right: a boxed in bed is flanked by a window and ledge on one side and wide closets on the other, which are hidden by the use of wood panels. Left of this section is the ample living room that shares the same space as the kitchen and dining area. Saturated with natural light that flows through the glass wall that opens out onto a small terrace, the room features a large plush sofa, a wall-mounted TV, and custom-built birchwood furniture, all against bare white walls. Vintage pieces include the dining chairs by William Plunkett and the original 1970s wool carpet purchased in Camden Town, London. The master bedroom and en suite bathroom are located behind a fixed partition made of wood and glass and a sliding door. This luminous volume filters natural light through a large window and artificial neon light from a false ceiling. Minimalist lines punctuated by stylistic design pieces and precise lighting compose this stylishly modern space.

Architect: UdA
Location: Nice, France
Completion Date: 1998
Area: 645 square feet
Photographs: Heiko Semeyer

A mix of modern and vintage furniture creates a stylishly elegant space.

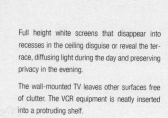

Full height white screens that disappear into recesses in the ceiling disguise or reveal the terrace, diffusing light during the day and preserving privacy in the evening.

The wall-mounted TV leaves other surfaces free of clutter. The VCR equipment is neatly inserted into a protruding shelf.

The dining table and chairs are by William Plunkett, London 1968. The table is a slender wood panel that rests on a solid steel frame and the floor is made of Bateig Azul stones from Alicante.

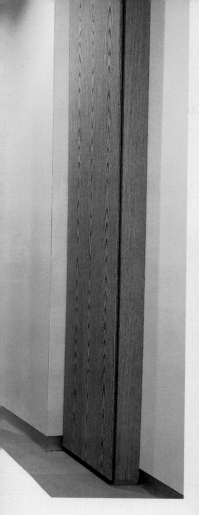

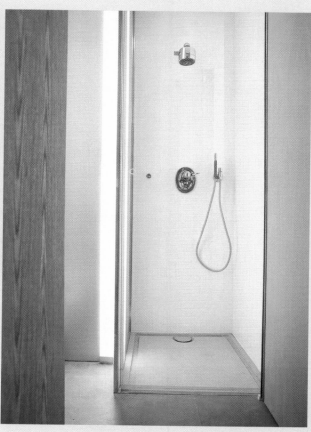

Flat in Nice

UdA

Located on the sixth floor of a 1950s building, this summer apartment, the backbone of which measures 6 feet wide and 97 feet long, runs long and narrow, with open views of the sea. The layout of rooms and open space is inspired by the interior features of a boat. On one side lies a 22-foot-wide living space, and on the other a 9-foot-wide corridor. On the north end is the master bedroom with its own bathroom and walk-in closet. The living room culminates on a terrace facing the water. The brilliant white lacquered wood surfaces hide a multitude of cupboards and a false ceiling emits indirect flourescent light. Such functional components as glass partitions, fixed and movable screens, and sliding doors contribute to the clean aesthetics and versatility of the space. From its visibility through the clear glass sinks in the bathrooms to the large-scale underwater images in laid glass partitions, water is a running motif throughout the apartment. In the studio, the bathroom is separated from the kitchen by an awesome transparency of a gigantic glass aquarium that lights up from behind.

Architect: UdA
Location: Nice, France
Completion Date: 2000
Area: 965 square feet
Photographs: Hervé Abbadie

This long and narrow apartment culminates in a terrace that offers spectacular views of the blue sea.

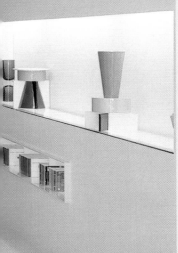

Wall niches act as shelves for original vases and other decorative objects.

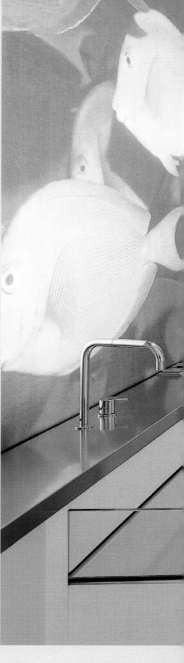

The streamlined kitchen is made of stainless steel. A transparent screen illuminates an enormous image of underwater fish. The table disappears into the wall to gain space.

Barcelona Residence

Cristina Algás and Patricio Martínez

The distribution of space and activity forms a major part of this attic redesigned for a young working couple with children. The areas within the home are arranged into places of activity. A fairly rectangular space holds a central area with the kitchen/dining room, living room, and bathroom, and on either end the children's room and terrace and the master bedroom. The unique aspect of this apartment is the visibility of certain elements, primarily the bathroom, located in front of the kitchen. Partly disguised by a curved corner of iroko wood panels that enclose the toilet, the washbasins and bathtub are exposed so that the parents, for example, can watch their child taking a bath without having to leave the kitchen while cooking. This aesthetic might be more common in ultra-modern spaces where bathroom fixtures are design pieces that form part of the creative concept; here, however, simple materials are exposed confidently without regard to taboos of design or privacy. In the same way, the rest of the space uses basic but hardwearing materials with both stylish and functional qualities. The floor is a continuous pavement coated in gray resin, a resistant and durable surface that is also an excellent insulator. Ample storage is provided through kitchen cupboards, space-saving elements, bookshelves, and the floor-to-ceiling iroko wood closets that also form a warm and neutral background for different kinds of furniture and decorative pieces.

Architects: Cristina Algás and Patricio Martínez
Location: Barcelona, Spain
Completion Date: 2000
Area: 965 square feet
Photographs: Jose Luis Hausmann

In this case, the idea of a center table was discarded so that the area felt more roomy. An entire wall space was used to fix shelves for books.

Large windows are always an advantage in small rooms and tight spaces.

The kitchen is the main character, playing a big role within the distribution and allocation of space.

A wall-mounted TV and a night table on wheels are versatile features in the small bedroom, which looks beyond a large window onto a private green garden.

White walls, glossy gray floors, plain white tiles, and warm iroko wood act as a modest background for plants, bright colors, and small details that adorn the space.

White House

Cristina Algás and Patricio Martinez

Small living spaces sometimes have to make do with only a single natural light source at the front or rear. In this case, there was only one room open to the facade windows that received direct sunlight, leaving the other rooms towards the back in shadow for most of the day. In order to correct this, without meddling with any structural walls, the architects opened out the frontal area by eliminating partitions creating a spacious L-shaped living room, kitchen, and dining area. The layout was cleverly structured so that the living room is visible from the kitchen but the kitchen slightly out of view from the living room. The corridor from which the front door and bedroom are accessed was designed wider in relation to the overall dimensions of the apartment so that as much daylight as possible is conducted through the hallway to the bedroom in the rear. Forming the perimeter of the bedroom are flush closets that read as clean, uninterrupted surfaces. The en suite bathroom, which lies in front of the bed on the other side of the corridor, is a continuation of the bedroom unless the large sliding door is closed. The decoration is simple, comfortable, and functional, with mainly neutral colors, plain white walls, light parquet, and plenty of cupboards and closets for storage. The kitchen counter doubles as a breakfast table or snack area. Alongside, a whole wall of shelves holds books, ornaments, and frames that add to the practical decoration of the apartment.

Architects: Cristina Algás and Patricio Martinez
Location: Barcelona, Spain
Completion Date: 2000
Area: 1,000 square feet
Photographs: Jose Luis Hausmann

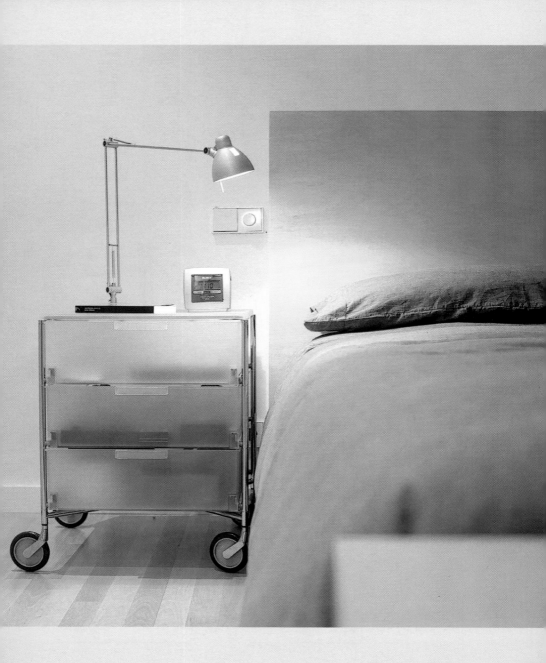

Design on wheels: keeping furniture mobile is essential within small spaces to make circulation more flexible.

In the living room, a distinguished design piece:
the Zig Zag Stoel by Gerrit Rietvelsd from 1934.

Matching bench and headboard offer an extra surface for clothes or decorative objects. The wheeled night tables also provide storage and their translucency gives a sense of weightlessness.

The bathroom and bedroom consist of a continuous space, separated by a large sliding white door that when shut disappears into the surrounding flush closets.

Mini House

Atelier Bow Wow

Located within a dense residential district in a very urban precinct, this residential space is much like the rest of Tokyo's architectural sites: very small. In a response to its fluid and unstable environment, the architects offset the building from each site limit and pushed out sub-volumes towards the fenceless boundaries. The fine steel structure fully utilizes the perimeter walls and floors of the building, doing away with any overriding post-and-beam framework. This gave architects the liberty to make openings in or protrusions out of the structural surface. One of these protrusions on the front side creates a space underneath the elevation that acts as a garage for the car. Stone steps lead to the entrance located at the side of the house, from where the three floor are visible. They are linked by way of a staircase with a continuous geometric handrail that changes angles. The basement floor consists of a storage room opposite the main structure. The staircase doubles as storage space by having extended each step into a shelf. On the ground floor, the entrance leads to a living room and kitchen on the left and a bathroom on the right. The kitchen was lowered to distinguish it from the living area. Upstairs on the first floor is the main bedroom and two small balconies on the front and lateral side. Large windows punctuate the walls, and inside the walls are fully used for storage, keeping the rooms remarkably uncluttered despite the limited space they dispose of.

Architect: **Atelier Bow Wow**
Location: **Tokyo, Japan**
Completion Date: **1997**
Area: **815 square feet**
Photographs: **Shigeru Hiraga**

Imagination and practicality must be employed when designing a small living space. Here, a staircase doubles as a shelf unit.

Open garage: A mini finds shade under an extension of Mini House.

Tokyo Residence

Makiko Tsukada

Located in a residential area in Tokyo, this small two-story house is constructed almost entirely of timber. The main accommodation block consists of library shelving made of laminated plywood and timber that runs along the north and south walls on both levels. On the ground floor, the bedroom lies underneath a corridor, making it a comfortable, quiet area. Six paper sliding doors envelop the room, their translucency filtering natural light into the space. Some allow access to the corridor while others are closets. This creates a flexibility of space that permits the bedroom to be divided into small rooms and also for the space to be used from both sides of the doors. The living room is found on the first floor, an open area in which light and air pass fluidly from one side to another. The room faces a large open terrace on one side, and has windows on the other walls. Light wood composes the minimalist interiors of this space, influenced by Asian characteristics and barely furnished to accentuate the enhanced spaciousness often longed for within small urban spaces.

Architect: Makiko Tsukada
Location: Tokyo, Japan
Completion Date: 1999
Area: 1,000 square feet
Photographs: Mitsumasa Fujitsuka

Narrow spaces can be used to make a small studio or office space.

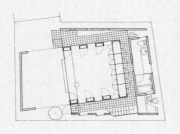

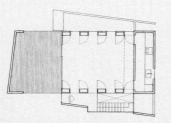

The living area looks out onto a long terrace that opens by way of glass sliding doors.

The pillars in front of the staircase conceal shelves to store books and other objects. Hallways are fit with cupboards and storage units, and the space underneath the stairs is used to accommodate a small studio.

Apartment in Antwerp

Vincent Van Duysen Architects

The object of the design of this apartment was to use the existing structure of the two areas that make up the apartment and instill a more open and spacious atmosphere. These two parts were defined as day and night areas. The day area consists of the living and dining room and has no formal entrance, while the night area is made up of the bedroom and bathroom, located along a central corridor that opens completely through the use of full height sliding doors. On one side a washbasin and an open shower area transform this section of the hallway into a large white bathroom. On the other end, the bedroom is finished in dark tinted oak with dove gray walls, granting a more intimate and warm atmosphere. The border between the day and night zones is amplified by a long glass wall that, instead of reducing the space, actually makes it look larger. The kitchen is composed of a block made of white stone and a kitchen unit against the wall finished in dark brown wood. Suspended over the island is a rectangular lamp that mimics its shape and color. The ample living room is divided by a large supporting pillar; a long dining table and armchair are to its left and in front of the kitchen, while the sitting and reading area rests comfortably over large rugs and carpets to its right. Maximum light, pure architecture, and natural tones, combined with different art pieces and secondhand furniture, produce a modern, refined, and unpretentious style.

Architect: Vincent Van Duysen Architects
Location: Antwerp, Belgium
Completion Date: 2001
Area: 1,000 square feet
Photographs: Jan Verlinde

The large cloister table is secondhand and offers a more raw texture to the space.

Unusual lamps and artwork can add visual interest to a space without the need of bright colors or designer furniture.

The glass doors are marked by square black panes that stand out against the white walls beyond, creating an interaction with the black frames that hang in the hallway.

The bathroom area is found along a hallway and
can be joined or separated by large sliding doors.

New York Apartment

Arthur de Mattos Casas

Home to the architect who designed it, this apartment is located in New York City. He uses the space as his residence whenever he is not working in Brazil. This practical apartment consists of a living room linked to the dining area, one bedroom, one bathroom, a kitchen, and a studio. The principal feature is the living/dining room that links to a continuous space that can be closed off by sliding doors. The resulting smaller room includes a corner desk that rests against the window, as well as a sofa bed, allowing the area to be used as a private guest bedroom. Evoking the passion of his home country, red is the principal color used throughout the space, combined with neutral tones of cream and gray. A large mirror is placed on one side of the living room to enhance the illusion of space. On the other side, a sleek black dining table is backed by a long, narrow abstract painting that lengthens the space. The bedroom is decorated warmly and receives plenty of natural light. Shelves and tables solve any problems of limited space. Most of the furniture was designed by the architect and manufactured in Brazil, including the living room rug made on a hand-loom. The apartment offers a practical, comfortable, and pleasurable residence for this Brazilian-based architect.

Architect: Arthur de Mattos Casas
Location: New York, US
Completion Date: 1998
Area: 980 square feet
Photographs: Tuca Reinés

Dark furniture against light walls makes an attractive contrast in small interiors.

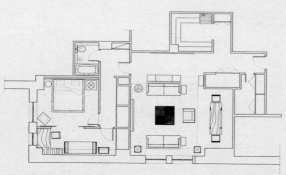

Closets all along the hallway provide the necessary storage. The living areas are defined by a change in flooring.

The living room space seems to double when a large mirror is introduced.

The bedroom features a long, rich dark-brown panel behind the bed that acts as a surface for a row of small photographs in large dark frames.

A Japanese-style table with matching benches is paired up with transparent chairs on either side.

Residence in Vienna

Pool Architektur

This project is located on the terrace of an old industrial building in Vienna. Pool Architektur, a young and daring Austrian team, managed to transform the building's water tank into a micro-apartment. The result is an example of how a true home can be created in only 194 square feet. The architects preserved the watertank's original structure, including the sloping walls on the lower part. Though they painted the brick white, they did not smooth it out or rejoin it in order to maintain its rough texture. The glass facade that leads onto the terrace provides the apartment with views of the city's rooftops. Most of the furniture, including the bed, the dining table, and the closet, is mobile and slides into a small metal volume in the wall when not in use. This storage volume sticks out of the construction and enables the residents to free up space inside. The kitchen projects out of the wall and is a sculptural element made of a metal sheet in the form of an L. The refrigerator is suspended from the ceiling and is strategically positioned to facilitate its use without blocking the passageway. The architects did not hang curtains because the one space that requires privacy, the bathroom, is closed off. A rotating television sits in a nook in the wall and can be turned towards either the bathroom or the living room. Pool Architektur has demonstrated that claustrophobia does not result from a home's measurements, but from poor management of space.

Architect: **Pool Architektur**
Location: **Vienna, Austria**
Completion Date: **1999**
Area: **194 square feet**
Photographs: **Hertha Hurnaus**

No more magazines: A pivoting TV in the bathroom is the "ultimate statement in contemporary bathroom design.

Clever distribution and the use of mobile furniture creates not only the illusion but also an actual gain of space in the least likely places.

A television on a rotating metallic platform is inserted into the wall and can be turned either towards the bathroom or towards the living area and the bedroom.

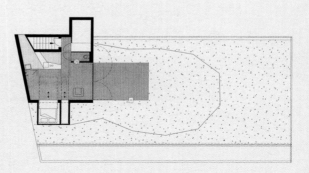

Duplex in Stockholm

Claesson Koivisto Rune Arkitektkontor

This project features the downtown Stockholm apartment of an architect who forms part of this Swedish team. Since the client is also one of the firm's designers, the space embodies the group's precepts: continuity between spaces, exquisite constructional details and serene ambiences with sparks of color. Due to the apartment's small size, 763 square feet, the architects avoided the use of doors, except in the foyer and bathroom. Though the partitions between the spaces run the entire height of the apartment, they do not quite touch the ceiling. This creates a relationship between rooms that enables the house to be perceived as a unit, like a collection of organic spaces. The communal areas, the living room, dining room, bathroom and kitchen, are located on the first floor. The partition wall that separates the dining room from the living room supports a set of stairs that leads to the upper level, where a small studio and a bedroom are located. The bedroom has access to a terrace with views of the city. As with most of their projects, the young architects used limited materials in the apartment: light wood for the floors and furniture, a glazed mosaic in the bathroom and kitchen, a wool rug in the private zones and bright colors on some of the walls. Minerals collected in the Arizona desert inspired the project's tonalities. The team, which also specializes in industrial design, combined various furnishings and design objects with pieces of their own creation.

Architects: Claesson Koivisto Rune Arkitektkontor
Location: Stockholm, Sweden
Completion Date: 2000
Area: 763 square feet
Photographs: Patrick Engquist

The staircase is supported by a partition wall, which enables it to occupy a very small space.

The bedroom occupies the top floor of an old building with sloping walls. In order to tone down the lack of usable space, the architects installed windows that run along the wall and continue towards the roof.

The windows lift the ceiling and introduce light and views.

Images of the partitions that separate the spaces. The layout of the walls eliminates the need for doors, maintaining privacy without losing continuity.

Coarse wooden beams painted white entrance
the height of the attic.

Flat in Sydney

William Smart Architects

The layout of this apartment, located on Australia's famous Bondi Beach, is organized around a pivoting dining table. The table rotates 180 degrees from the kitchen, past the studio and to the living room. It turns around a column that replaced the original structural wall. The structural system, made of stainless steel, supports a glass plate that is ten feet long and weighs 220 pounds. To facilitate the table's movement, the work zone can be closed off with sliding fabric panels that offer privacy. The bedroom also has sliding doors made of translucent, bluish resin, which enable the residents to enjoy views of the sea from the bed. An electronically activated video projection ensures darkness at night by blocking the light that passes through the translucent panels. The materials used in the apartment differ in luminosity and translucency in order to emphasize the impact of the views. Since there is hardly any frontier between the interior and the exterior spaces, seasonal and climactic changes dominate the apartment's character. Though this home includes a complete music system, more than sixty points of light and the latest in television and video technology, the careful design of these installations creates a peaceful atmosphere. A good example of the architects' skill for details is the large piece of white furniture that stores all the kitchen appliances and electronic apparatus, leaving the living room free of objects.

Architect: William Smart Architects
Location: Sydney, Australia
Construction date: 1999
Area: 538 square feet
Photographes: Gene Raymond Ross

The living room is streamlined with the careful, thorough concealment of electric appliances and storage.

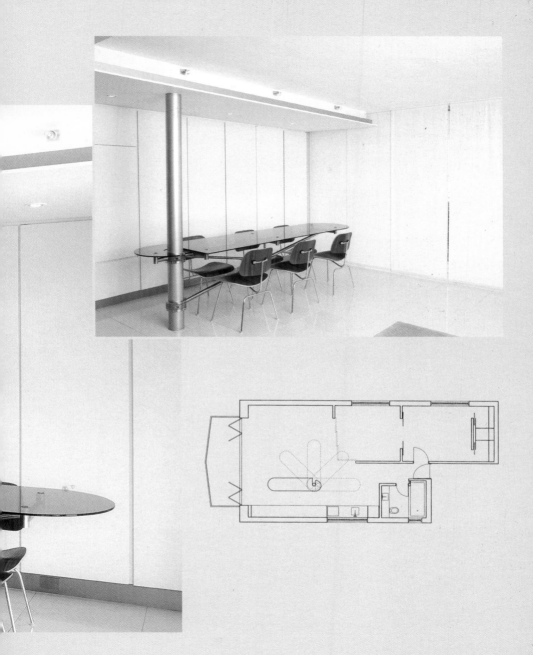

The bedroom and living room are connected by a window that offers views of the bay from the bed.

A pivoting table is the star feature of this apartment, permitting its function to become variable: a surface for the kitchen, dining area, or living room.

Milan Apartment

Marco Savorelli

This project entailed the restoration of an attic apartment in the historic center of Milan. The 968-square-foot space was transformed into a modern, sophisticated, and elegant loft. The general concept was to integrate all the rooms into a single space, thus avoiding doors and interior partitions. The choice of only one type of flooring, dark hardwood, also contributes to a feeling of unity. The floor's tone contrasts with the clean, white walls and inclined ceilings. The client and architect worked closely together throughout the project and opted to start from scratch. They followed abstract concepts that enabled the residence to evolve during the renovation process. The property's old functions were replaced with useful, simple, and innovative forms. Keeping in mind the sloped ceilings, the architect created a principal axis of circulation in the center of the dwelling, where the ceilings are the highest. The spaces for activities related to leisure or relaxation were constructed in the perimeter. The service areas, like the bathroom, the kitchen, and the cabinets, are monolithic volumes. When reduced to simple forms, they become works of plastic art that amplify spatial perception. While functional, the design is teetering on the edge of irony and provocation. Since this attic apartment is a clear succession of spaces with no defined frontiers, the entryway becomes the living room and the bedroom melts into the bathroom and the kitchen.

Architect: Marco Savorelli
Location: Milan, Italy
Completion Date: 1999
Area: 960 square feet
Photographs: Matteo Piazza

The furniture here shares a common language:
Low, linear, and minimal.

A kitchen island visually isolates the kitchen from the living room.

Sloping ceilings make this minimalist space feel more intimate.

Even the shower is left open to view. This transparent volume is a decorative statement on its own.

Apartment in Turin

The commission was to remodel a dark, empty attic on the fourth floor of an eighteenth-century building in the baroque center of Turin, Italy. They chose to organize it on two levels with a total surface area of just under 960 square feet. This resulted in orderly living quarters with a vertical layout of rooms and the domestic functions. On the lower level they placed two bedrooms with their respective bathrooms and a storage closet. The upper level contains space for daytime activities: the kitchen, a pantry, the living room, and the dining room. All these spaces, except that used for storage, are integrated into a single unit. This increases the perception of the house's size. The multivalent apartment is, moreover, lighted by a large window that keys open by way of an electrical device to provide light for the lower level. The staircase joining the two levels is the project's nerve center. It connects the two levels and increases the flow of natural light. The metal frame holds up, birch steps without risers in the first flight, and sandblasted glass ones the second flight. The whole element is supported by a double-height partition that includes a birch bookcase. The choice of materials brings out the connection between the spaces, for example, the use of glass partitions in place of walls. The heavy wooden beams used in the original construction have also been replaced by light metal pieces that increase the usable height.

Architect: **UdA**
Location: **Turin. Italy**
Completion Date: **1997**
Area: **960 square feet**
Photographs: **Emilio Conti**

Floating planes of glass produce a buoyant sensation, especially through the glass-step staircase.

The upper level, which contains the kitchen, the dining room, and the living room, was designed to be perceived as an attic that does not take up the whole condominium.

The transparent material of the handrails makes it possible to view full dimensions of the two levels from the attic.

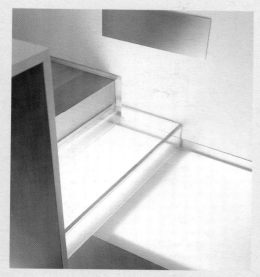

The absence of risers in the steps and the materials used in the staircase turn it into an ethereal element that does not interrupt the fluidity of the space.

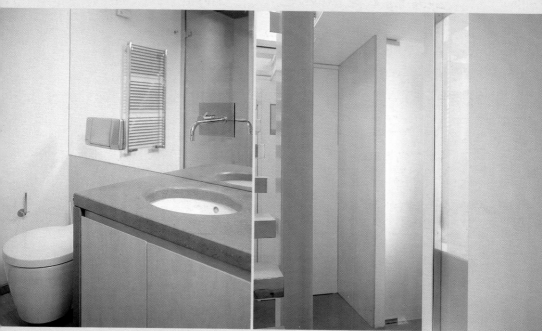

The stairs lead to the upper level, which contains the kitchen, dining room, and living room.

The upper level was designed around the concept of an attic, so as to take up the least space possible from the whole condominium.

Barcelona Apartment

Jorge Rangel

The design of this living space unifies the concepts of loft and apartment. A raw shell space was taken, its pillars and brick surfaces left intact, and converted into a multiuse dwelling where living, eating, cooking, and socializing take place within one shared area. Unlike in many lofts, the sleeping area can be closed off by doors, thus maintaining the privacy that a small loft like this one could not have otherwise. The living area is more or less divided from the kitchen and dining area by a visual distinction—a vaulted brick roof. This original structure was kept exposed over the cooking and eating areas, and to play up this feature, a brick kitchen counter was raised to serve as an extra worktop, a snack table, or bar. Light is a major asset in this space, thanks to the set of large windows that surround the facade and also part of the bedroom, which also lets light in from the living room through a window placed above the doors. High ceilings further magnify the sense of spaciousness. Kitchen cupboards, a hidden pantry, and a corner closet offer useful storage space, and the living room table made to measure incorporates an extra surface for magazines and books. The main colors are given by lamp shades, table tops, and unique chairs, such as the red chaise longue by NIPIU, a Mario Olivera design. Different kinds of spotlighting also illuminate the space. In short, a typical raw loft space, smaller than most, with the advantage of a closed-off, initimate bedroom.

Stylist: **Jorge Rangel**
Location: **Barcelona. Spain**
Completion Date: **2000**
Area: **840 square feet**
Photographs: **Jose Luis Hausmann**

Each area is defined by a certain element: The living room by a floor carpet, the kitchen by the brick counter, and the dining area by the vaulted ceilings.

The large kitchen counter adds color and plenty
of space to prepare meals.

Colorful and orginal details give a space character. Light is also an important factor to be exploit-
ed in any living space.

Maximalist in Barcelona

Mauro Pelizzari

This first floor apartment reflects the many facets and qualities of the area in which it resides. The rich mixture of faces, cultures, and sensations offered by the gothic quarter of Barcelona are what inspire the multifaceted nature of this space. The extremely tall ceilings prompted architects to create a mezzanine level so as to take better advantage of the available space. The entrance consists of a double-height foyer with exposed eighteenth-century wooden beams, a tall mirror, and a hanging crystal chandelier. A small hallway leads to a dramatic sitting area, dining room, and kitchen. The bohemian-style living room, more like a chill-out area, displays a variety of different textures, colors, and lighting techniques. Opposite, a slightly more contemporary setting: a long, narrow table accompanied by a bench on either side, upholstered in a deep red velvet and an industrial-style kitchen in stainless steel. A unique tunnel-shaped extractor is suspended from the ceiling over the stove. Separating the kitchen from the rest of the space is a lavish red velvet drape. An iron-clad staircase leads up to the mezzanine level, which serves as another relaxation area and to its left, a cozy bedroom with views of the exposed beams. An eclectic mix of styles make up this theatrical setting that is neither overcharged nor uncomfortable—a balance between exotic and modern aesthetics that work together within a limited space.

Architect: Mauro Pelizzari
Stylist: Jorge Rangel
Location: Barcelona, Spain
Completion Date: 2000
Area: 860 square feet
Photographs: Jose Luis Hausmann

An extravagant chandelier hangs from the high ceiling, forming an excellent contrast with the rough old ceiling beams.

Minimalism takes a step back: Elaborate patterns, shapes, and colors can also work well inside small spaces.

The table was designed to serve as a dining table as well as a surface for cooking and preparation. A steel cabinet with etched glass door used as a pantry to keep kitchen materials.

Decorative details in the bedroom, foyer, and bathroom—such as the mirror frames, chairs, and curtains—have clearly rococo and classical influences. These elements are subtly intertwined with contemporary lighting and other materials.

Oasis in London

Gabriella Szulman

Despite its relatively small size and its division into separate rooms, this apartment was essentially hand-crafted by its artistic owner, now a practicing ceramicist in London. Having bought the apartment in a state of disrepair, Gabriella Szulman took down all the existing wallpaper, tiles, and paint and put up an invigorating assortment of patterns, designs, and colors. Instead of taking the minimalist approach to limited space, she strategically chose colors and placed objects that create atmosphere while utilizing space. In the entrance hallway, an aged wooden trunk also serves as a surface for decorative objects. Hanging above it, an intricatelysewn wall hanging of fabric and pebbles. The walls in the living areas are painted in oranges and mustards, and a light violet in the bedrooms. The kitchen is functional and has a very homey feeling. There is no need to hide glasses, utensils, or containers. In fact, they give character to the space. Gabriela opted for a more neutral beige in this case. A myriad of turquoise and gold swirls inundate the bathroom. Its white, handmade tiles balance the presence of color and allow the small area to breathe. To gain space, a variety of shelves and hooks, as well as a useful apparatus were hung over the bath. The latter is used to hang towels and hinges open to serve as a clothesline for drying laundry. Another example of how to decorate a home imaginatively without the need of expensive materials or extensive open space.

Interior Design: **Gabriella Szulman**
Location: **London, UK**
Completion Date: **1995**
Area: **805 square feet**
Photographs: **Carlos Dominguez**

Imagination and creativity liven up a small space and make it functional in unique ways.

Scattered objects, wall-hanging glasses, and pictures on cupboards, make this a warm and inviting kitchen.

The many fabrics, vases, and paintings displayed around the home are part of the owner's collections gathered from her work and travels to places like Argentina, Cuba, and Brazil. The variety of tones harmonize rather than clash in the multi-colored rooms.

London Flat

Kim Pooley

This apartment unveils a brazen collection of daring colors, patterns, and styles, unusually lively for a London interior. The space is divided into several rooms: An entrance hall; a rectangular living and dining room, separated by an intricately carved Oriental bureau; a small kitchen; and a master bedroom and bath. A marked oriental influence is present, both in the colors and materials used. Various rugs, dark furniture, velvety couches, and roughly painted walls in deep reds and vivid yellows predominate. Wall sconces and spotlights brighten the living room and, in the bedroom matching lamps sit on the night tables, one of which is a shelf fixed to the wall. The kitchen is somewhat rustic, with curious vintage appliances like the hanging clock and the 1950s radio box. The bathroom, with its relaxing free-standing bathtub and sultry atmosphere, is the ideal place to take a steaming candlelit bath. Flowers, candles, silk pillows, and paintings decorate the space, each element thoughtfully placed without losing its carefree and bohemian air. The intense colors, balanced by the natural light from the large windows and terrace doors, offer a tempting invitation inside—and away from the brisk London weather.

Architect: Kim Pooley
Interior Design: Kim Pooley
Location: London, UK
Completion Date: 1999
Area: 965 square feet
Photographs: Carlos Dominguez

Mirrors can be used to perceptually enlarge a room. This one is framed in a light color to contrast with the dark walls.

Intricate details add warmth and personality to a home. This apartment radiates color and energy.

Vintage objects like the free-standing tub and the wall mounted first-aid kit add charm to this bathroom.

Shelves can serve as alternatives to night tables.

SANOID

FIRST AID

Apartment in California
Richard Aldredge ∘ Associates

This guest house studio is located half a block away from the Venice boardwalk and forms part of an existing three-story residence, linked together by a wooden bridge. The studio consists of a living area, sleeping alcove, and small bath. The exposed joist ceiling slants from a height of seven feet in the corner to seventeen feet on the south wall. It is punctuated by a north-facing skylight that illuminates the entire room. Corner windows afford views of the boardwalk and the beach. On the opposite side, an alcove looks down on the garden between the studio and the main residence. The eclecticism of the neighborhood is reflected in this building's design along with the studio's interior. The facade facing Sunset Court alley is broken into distinct and at times fragmentary elements, each in a specific material and color that establishes an intimacy and familiarity between pedestrian and architecture. On the other side the garden facade is also composed of distinct elements that make the outdoor space comfortably scaled. Inside, white walls and wood are a backdrop for a mix of styles that hint at a Native American influence. While the exterior exhibits a robust and linear quality, the interior maintains a feeling of retreat.

Architect: Richard Aldredge ∘ Associates
Photographer: Tom Bonner Photography
Location: Venice, California, US
Completion Date: 2001
Area: 500 square feet
Photographs: Tom Bonner Photography

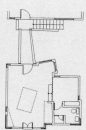

Interior design: These end tables are designed by
the architect in charge of the project.

The studio is accessed by a wooden bridge that
looks over the back garden.

Apartment in Munich

Form Werkstatt

This space located in Munich's historic center forms part of an old sewing machine factory. The architect in charge undertook the design to turn it into her own home. The objective was to create a flexible space through the use of elemental materials and construction methods that would facilitate the rehabilitation. Five modular wooden panels hung from a metallic rail were used to divide the space. These panels reinforce the longitudinal perspective of the space while separating the public and private areas. If desired, the bedroom—defined by its wood floor—can be merged with the living and working room into one continuous area. The lounge and studio were placed nearest the facade to profit from this single entry of natural light. The panels also serve to control the light distribution. Original furniture was obtained from markets and thrift shops, such as the gas pump recycled to hold dishes and the office storage used to keep clothes. The opening of an existing dumbwaiter was used to incorporate a shelf into the wall. The concrete floor is a reminder of the space's industrial past, which along with the metal and wood, establishes a multifaceted atmosphere in this modestly reworked loft.

Architect: Siggi Pfundt / Form Werkstatt
Location: Munich, Germany
Completion Date: 1999
Area: 800 square feet
Photographs: Karin Hebmann / Artur

The central table, in the same tone as the birch plywood panels, combines with the furnishings in warm colors to create a cozy environment that conserves the characteristics of the industrial space.

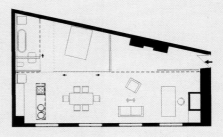

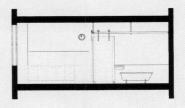

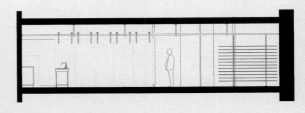

Hong Kong Apartment

Gary Chang / EDGE [HK] LTD

The aim of this project was to transform the space into a home that despite its limited porportions, would also serve as a place for leisure and entertainment. In order to take advantage of the light that enters through the back window, the bathroom, kitchen, and washing areas were grouped at the front, leaving the remaing space free to incorporate a multifunctional environment. Bedroom, living room, studio, and projection room coexist in this single small space. To achieve this, a combination of manipulated lighting techniques, lightweight divisions, and mobile furniture was employed. Work elements like books, videos, records, and personal areas like the wardrobe are concealed behind plain white curtains that can be easily open and closed. Translucent white materials and changes in ambient light give the space a weightless, uncluttered feel. To enhance this effect and deepen the space vertically, flourescent white tubes trail the floor and intense lights accentuate structural features. One of the few elements preserved from the original structure is the cherry wood tower that houses the projector, refrigerator, kitchen, bathroom, and washing machine. The window opening is also multifunctional: an extendable screen offers a surface for TV, video, and Internet. The combination of techniques and materials used to take maximum advantage of this miniature living space generate a unique, modern, and most theatrical home.

Architect: **Gary Chang / EDGE [HK] LTD**
Location: **Hong Kong, China**
Completion Date: **2000**
Area: **320 square feet**
Photographs: **Almond Chu**

Living areas take precedence over service areas in small living spaces. Leisure and entertainment require more space than kitchen or bathroom activities.

A clever positioning of elements allows for an opening in the bathroom in order to filter in natural light from the back window.

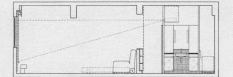
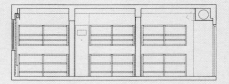

New York Loft

Alexander Gorlin

This loft is located in the Tribeca neighborhood of New York, in a building with a triangular layout that was previously used as an industrial and warehouse space. The architect Alexander Gorlin designed a floor plan that permitted the clearing and visual continuity of the entire facade. Inside the apartment, the architect used diverse forms and played with a combination of colors. The wall that divides the private areas—the library, the master bedroom, the closet, and the bathroom—from the social zone consists of a single organic form, with a circular design in the color red. The wall crosses the entire space along a diagonal. This gesture incorporates a winding staircase that leads to the roof garden, which allows natural light to shine down on the loft. The stainless steel kitchen cabinets emphasize cleanliness and reflect the light of the adjoining windows. A work island repeats the triangular form of the apartment's design. Along the same lines, and taking advantage of the light from the windows, the architect used a table and some chairs to define the living area, where a chimney and shelves for music equipment are built into the wall. Primary colors form dividing lines whose lively tones contrast. The rest of the white walls lighten the meeting of forms and colors. In this renovation, the architect made the most of a triangular floor plan with difficult proportions. The volumetric gesture enriches the space and takes full advantage of the light.

Architect: Alexander Gorlin
Location: New York, US
Completion Date: 1997
Area: 1,247 square feet
Photographes: Peter Aaron (Esto)

Warm colors and patterns remove the need for many decorative objects.

The kitchen island was triangle shaped to fit into a triangular space, leaving enough room for movement around the kitchen.

Partially isolated on one end of the space, the living room continues, occupying the length of the apartment.

Paris Apartment

Stephanie and Olivier

The design of this space was led by Stephanie, an illustrator and decorator, and Olivier, a graphic designer. Avid craftspeople, the couple went out in search of old furniture, spare parts, and vintage objects around the streets and in the well known flea markets of Paris. Every single item they chose was recycled with endless imagination and a great sense of humor. In such a small space, these two managed to fit a bedroom, living room, bathroom, bar, and even a sewing corner. The bedroom, painted in blue, is separated from the living room by a curtain made from plastic bags from the Belleville market, a fruit store in Paris. A map adorns the wall and a carpet from Brazil covers the floor. Located at the far end of the bedroom is the bathroom. In the living room, a sofa constructed from wooden transport pallets is decorated with a table cloth and cushions by Robert Le Héros. Above the sofa two suspended shelves serve as a library. Lamps have been crafted from an old radiator and a vacuum cleaner motor, and CDs are stored in wooden boxes next to the TV, painted in a vibrant yellow. Recycled wood was used to make the coffee table, and the standing lamp was created out of cable and a 1950s hair dryer. For the kitchen area a bar was erected out of bricks, and the countertop was fabricated from wooden panels that were nailed and varnished. Cans, bags, plastic flowers, anything imaginable was recycled and hand crafted to decorate this vibrant mini apartment.

Interior Designers: **Stephanie and Olivier**
Location: **Paris. France**
Completion Date: **2000**
Area: **409 square feet**
Photographs: **Vincent Leroux**

Taking advantage of small corners allows room for a studio. This one has been turned into a cozy sewing corner.

A secondhand oval frame, turned into an electric sunflower by placing light bulbs around its edge, is used to frame pictures.

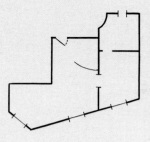

The curtain that divides the kitchen and living room was made out of plastic bags cut into large pieces and sewn together. The top was rolled around a wooden bar fixed to the wall.

Manual labor: The owners mixed cement, sand and water to seal the bricks together, and the walls are decorated with Stephanie's colored drawings printed onto leaves of Canson paper.

Nautical Loft

Cecconi Simone Inc.

This project is the smallest of three model apartments that were created for the restoration of an old warehouse in downtown Toronto. The container's form is reminiscent of naval constructions, and some design elements were inspired by the nautical theme, such as curtains made out of sails, boat lights and metallic stairs. One objective was to convey the spirit of the original building. The space conserves the authentic columns and the exposed steel ceiling. Only the floor was sanded down in the kitchen and covered with wood in the sleeping area. Since there was so little surface area available, the designers optimized the apartment's height by creating distinct levels. They used the inside of the platforms for storage and placed closets in the upper part that can be reached by stairs. They also hung sliding doors that can manipulate the space. Enormous sliding panels close off the bedroom at night and create a continuous space during the day. The partition walls in the bathroom are made of glass in order to provide natural illumination. Cecconi Simone designed various objects specifically for the loft, including the stairs that also serve as a towel bar in the bathroom, the lights, the kitchen cabinets, and the bed that features hangers on both sides and drawers on the inside. This project won a prestigious prize from Ontario's Interior Designers Association.

Architects: **Cecconi Simone Inc.**
Location: **Toronto, Canada**
Completion Date: **1997**
Area: **623 square feet**
Photographs: **Joy von Tiedemann**

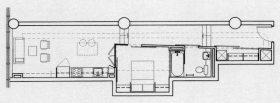

An en suite bathroom is visible through large glass doors that lead to the master bedroom.

A screen sustained by thin cables is casually loosened, elegantly revealing views of the city through a large living room window.

Projects

This chapter is dedicated to architectural proposals that have not yet been materialized. Drawing, plans and concepts are the basis for their evolution and are shown here to visualize the final product and to understand the ideas behind each project.

Aronoff house

Eric Owen Moss

The site of the present house is a narrowing strip bounded by a slope in the direction of the Santa Monica Mountains Conservancy, a 4,886 acre natural reserve within a much larger protected district. The singular structure can be explored, examined, and used as a lookout point because of its location and the configuration of the apartments. The windows maximize the spectacular and varied vistas of the surrounding forest.

The project includes, in addition to the residential areas, a studio, an office, and an apartment.

It is situated in a transitional zone on a the upper part of the site, adjacent to the southeastern boundaries of the property. On the highest of the three floors is the studio/office of the owners. The second floor has an office for three employees; the lowest floor is appointed as a private apartment for the father of one of the owners. The roof, facing the Resource Conservation District of the Santa Monica Mountains and the San Fernando Valley, was built of wood and also has different levels. There are therefore several open-air levels, and they are connected by way of a perimeter stairway as well as an interior stairway to the third floor.

The house was conceived to emerge from a conical section at the foot of a hill, combining spherical and cubical shapes. These interrelate in a complicated pattern, but they define a very advanced way of building.

Architect: Eric Owen Moss
Location: Tarzana, California, U.S.A.
Construction Date: 2004
Photographs: Paul Groh, Micah Heimlich, Todd Conversano

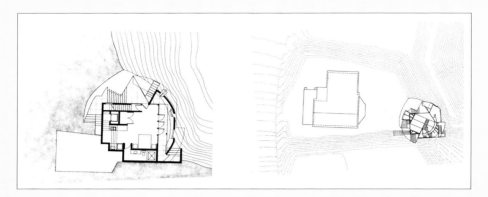

The design system of the roof was conceived as masonry arches that would formalize the roundness of the house.

The house emerges from a conical section at the foot of a hill, and combines spherical and cubical shapes.

Butterfly house

In 1996, Ed Lippmann was invited by a realtor to present the design for his future house on the outskirts of Sydney. Facing north, the place offers some spectacular panoramic views of the city and the harbor to the west.

The client insisted that the house should be subject to his belief in the principles ruling Feng Shui, the Chinese discipline that connects the spaces of a building directly with nature.

The two main curved forms distinguishing the structure pivot around a central body that defines the entranceway and which also contains the stairway that connects the six levels throughout the full trajectory of the house.

The west façade groups in a single unit the kitchen and the dining room on the ground floor along with a mezzanine living room. This area enjoys the best views of Sydney Harbor and simultaneously opens onto a patio garden with pool, dominating the west front of the site.

The building is a hybrid composition of concrete, steel, and glass. The concrete stiffens the horizontal structure of the steelwork. The metallic elements and an almost imperceptible aluminum section make way for the interface between each of the levels. They also open up the space to the large glass panels sheathing the piece.

Some of the most advanced technical systems have been used here to achieve the curved, sliding glass skin as well as the projecting cornices to protect from direct solar radiation while allowing heat accumulation and maximum natural lighting in all the spaces.

Architect: Lippmann Associates
Location: Sydney, Australia
Construction Date: 1998-2001
Photographs: Lippmann Associates

The rationale behind the intermediate form of the floor-to-floor layout is related to a smooth form of going up and down to harness the different views and energies in the immediate environment, including the best orientations toward the sun. The building is made of a concrete structure that uses large projecting cornices as terraces. The metallic parts of the sheathing interface with the concrete parts and support the large glass panels in the façades.

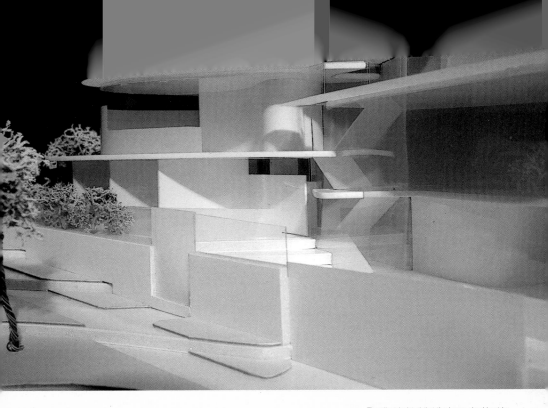

The client insisted that the house should not be subject to a design where straight lines were the norm because this did not correspond to his belief in the principles ruling Feng Shui.

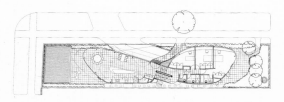

Access level

Plans of the study and the garage

Insideouthouse

Sandell Sandberg through Thomas Sandell. Pye Aurell

Insideouthouse is a living project conceived as a summer residence for a single person, couple, or family. From an architectural point of view, the house is on an open plan, with a labyrinthine character. One enters by way of a garden big enough to plant a tree in. The vestibule gives onto the porch and to the right is a large cabin-bedroom and two small ones. Another outside bathroom, which is smaller, gives onto the garden.

To the left of the entranceway is the kitchen and a dining area that looks onto one of the corners. Farther to the left, the living room opens out into the continually flowing space. The idea of the garden is to demarcate an exterior space and turn it into interior, blurring the boundary distinction. The garden creates an intimacy that does not depend on a context because the mobile bungalow is designed to be set into any location and thus adapts equally well to a Swedish woodland or to a place in the Alps or to the English countryside.

A wood-frame structure, it has painted wood façades with plastic elements. The untreated oak walls of the porch and of the outside bathroom continue on into the interior. Inside, the walls, ceiling, and floor are made of pine painted in white. The kitchen and the bath are tiled in white and the bathroom floor is white marble. Both the windows and the ceilings in the bedrooms are painted in yellow, blue, and orange.

Architect: **Sandell Sandberg through Thomas Sandell. Pye Aurell**
Initiator: **Wallpaper°**
Construction Date: **March 2000**
Photographs: **Tomasso Sartori**

The house is designed to be set into any location and thus adapts equally well to a Swedish woodland or to a place in the Alps or to the English countryside.

The house folds to create a small patio off which the other rooms open. The idea of the patio is to capture the landscape and bring it inside. This is the heart of the project's inside/outside game.

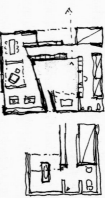

Basically designed for a couple, the house can accommodate guests in the small rooms arising out of the outer walls. The prototype was conceived by Tyler Brûlé, director of the magazine *Wallpaper*, and the architect Thomas Sandell during a barbecue at the journalist's house in Sweden.

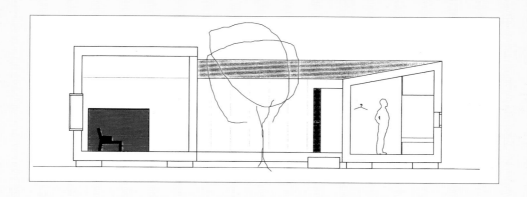

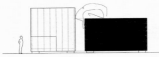

Belvedere Residence

Fougeron Architecture

In order to take advantage of the magificent views and integrate the house into the landscape, the siting is on a slightly inclined terrain. Two containing walls create a rise on which the living space is set, light and transparent.

The walls narrow the site and continue from the outside of the house to the inside. Wherever they are, they reinforce the relationship: the different levels are linked solidly both visually and physically.

On the back of the site, an excavation next to the first wall gives rise to a striking entranceway sequence backed up by the magnificent landscape gardening. Crossing the walkway over the garden in the direction of the main door, the proprietors will see themselves surrounded by trees, the sound of water along the garden wall, and views of the Golden Gate Bridge (through the translucent marble staircase).

The large volumes containing the dining room and the living room are located above the back wall. The floor-to-ceiling glass façade creates beautiful views. The glassed-in area containing the office is also slotted into this space, accessible from the interior staircase as well as the exterior walkway.

The office is on the third floor, which is also on grade level. The main living spaces are on the second floor, and the bedrooms are on the lowest level. All of these spaces are directly accessed from outside.

Architect: Fougeron Architecture
Location: Belvedere, California, U.S.A.
Construction Date: In design phase,
projected for 2002
Photographs: Fougeron Architecture
(maquette and renderings)

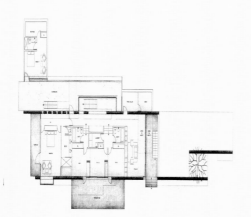

This belvedere, a California residence, a 6,458
square-foot design, is still in the design phase.

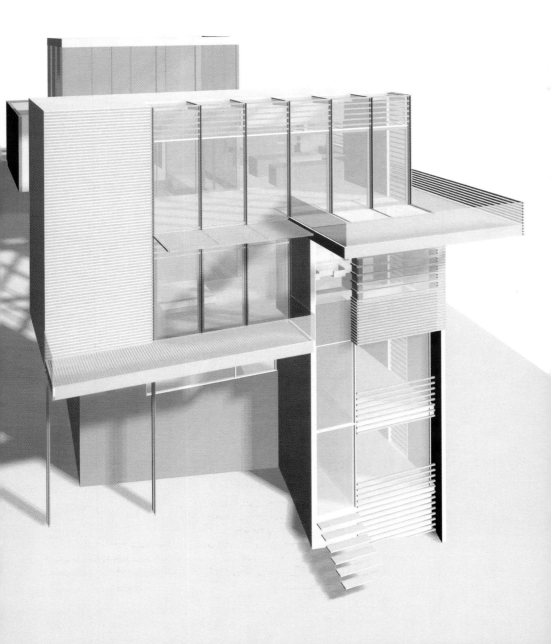

Beacon Street

Fougeron Architecture

Fougeron Architecture is a renowned North American firm whose work reveals a strong compromise by the clarity of its proposals, the integrity of its designs, and the quality of architectural details. The founder of the firm, the architect Anne Fougeron, seeks the perfect balance between the idea of architecture and the final form taken on by the constructed building. Her work, as may be seen in the Beacon Street House, can be defined by three basic premises: that the architectural space should be mod-ulated by the quality and the characteristics brought about by natural light; that any innovation applied to the structure should become architectural ornamentation; and, finally, that the exploration of the visual and tactical character of the materials should make its inhabitants able to enjoy the building.

The project consists in remodeling and extending a residence on a San Francisco hill. The building's conception is founded on three concepts: perpendicularity, transparency, and temporality.

The first concept is applied to the project by fitting the steep incline of the site on which the building is set by means of different mechanisms such as glass flooring, or a light stairway, tucked like an elevator into a glass shaft.

The transparency comes about when an invisible transition is produced between the interior space and the exterior of the dwelling. Temporal is the perception of the passage of time one has through the seasonal changes produced in the urban landscape.

Architect: **Fougeron Architecture**
Location: **Beacon Street. San Francisco. U.S.A.**
Construction Date: **2004**
Photographs: **Fougeron Architecture**

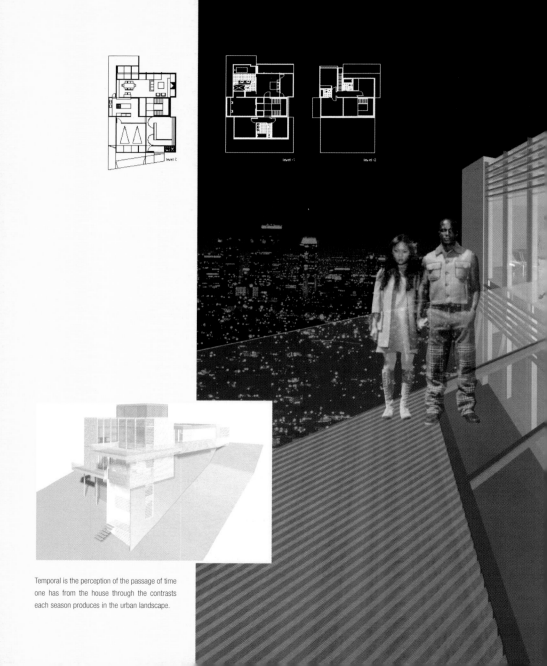

level 0   level -1   level -2

Temporal is the perception of the passage of time
one has from the house through the contrasts
each season produces in the urban landscape.

transparency

verticality

temporality

Floor 0   Floor 1   Floor 2

The access level of the house is on grade level,
where the day-use rooms are located (kitchen,
dining room, living room). The lower floor contains
the bedrooms.

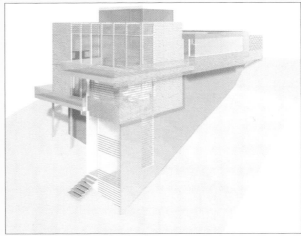

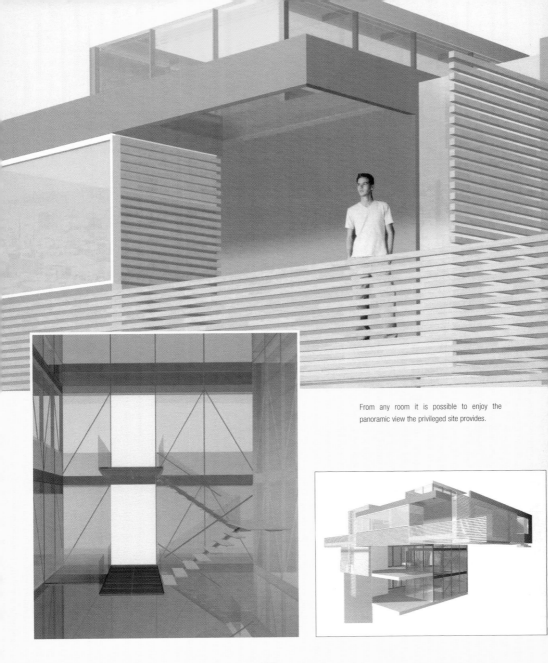

From any room it is possible to enjoy the panoramic view the privileged site provides.

Level 0: Entranceway, study, kitchen, dining room, living room

Level -1: General rooms and bathrooms

Level -2: Guest rooms and bathroom

Level -3: Gym and storeroom

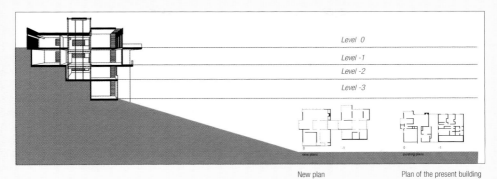

Level 0
Level -1
Level -2
Level -3

New plan

Plan of the present building

Wooster Street loft

Archetectonics

The Wooster Street project consisted of turning a fifth-floor apartment in a remodeled SoHo building into a living space for an art collector. The apartment that defines this project appears to be a loft, an existing and manipulable space. Doing it over again with additions and divisions meant reformulating the domestic elements for the creation of space flow and continuity.

The loft's design generated different zones with three uses stipulated: public, private, guest. And the general concept relates these concepts and links them. The division plans of the rooms become transparent, slippery, pivotal membranes. The kitchen is defined by a dividing wall that folds back and suspends the work surfaces. The molded aluminum of the walls turns into a kind of cabin modulation. Inside, we find two suspended, cornice-like work islands and a third fixed one of cement and polyurethane that turns on the breakfast pivot. The presence of a hearth as something with its own identity is separated from the wall and made the central visual focus.

The bathroom is a floating capsule whose functions are integrated to form a single sweeping element surrounded by glass panels. This supposes physical separations and no visual separations in the space, with showers that are seen and heard as such. Finally, the house contains fields with different functions, always retaining that continual flowing sweep of space, with the salient textures in what are screens more than walls.

Architect: Archetectonics
Location: Wooster Street, SoHo, New York, U.S.A.
Construction Date: 1998
Photographs: Paul Warchol

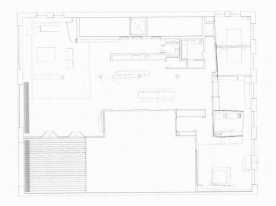

The Wooster Street project consisted of turning a fifth-floor apartment in a remodeled SoHo building into a living space for an art collector.

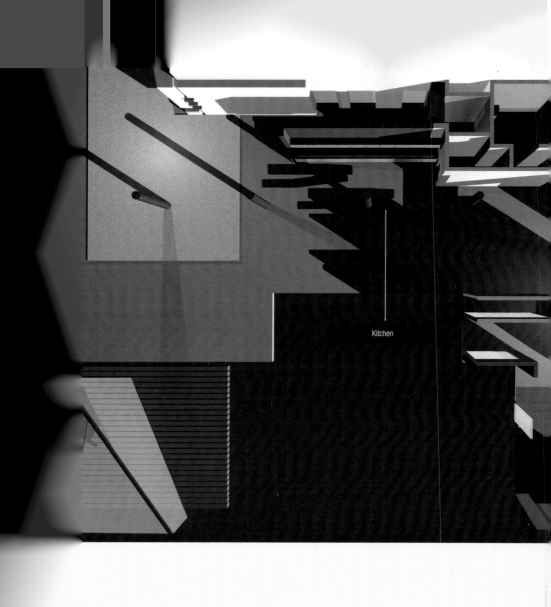

Kitchen

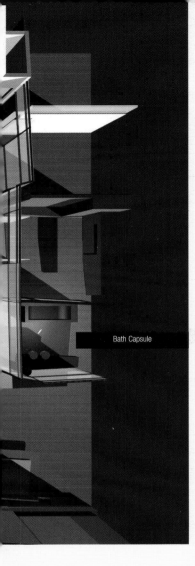

Bath Capsule

In the floor plan, the capsules may be appreciated in their function of making the bathrooms separate from the perimeter walls.

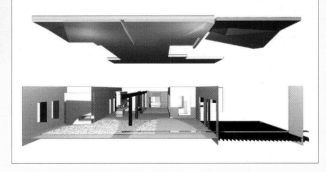

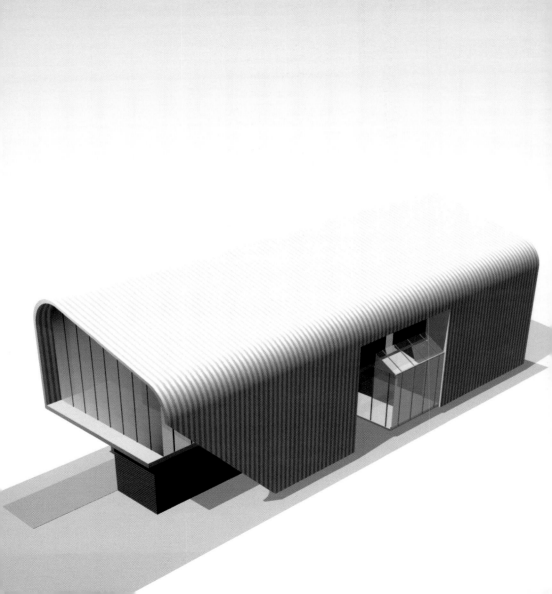

Rooftecture M

Barclay-Crousse Arquitectos

Rooftecture M is a project that suggests a chair shape for a house and workshop under construction in a small city three hours by train from Osaka, Japan, on a site that is not very large, but flat and in an attractive residential zone.

The ground plan of the house-workshop is rectangular, with rounded lines on the north and the south sides.

Including a workshop capable of handling a great influx of visitors was one of the initial requirements of the owner. This was the way in which the architects were requested to construct a series of spaces that would respect the quietness of the place and not attract attention from the street, in spite of the visits.

The workshop is in the northern section of the second floor, looking onto the street and located above the bathroom, the laundry room, and a second bathroom on the ground floor.

The dining room-living room is also on the ground floor, and has enough space to allow for comfortable family gatherings. This bay also admits abundant light and enjoys good ventilation.

The configuration of the house is due to the continuation, free of angles, of the lateral wall and the roof. This sweeping continuity in space is the architect's response to keeping it inside as a place for family meetings.

Architect: **Shuhei Endo Architect Institute**
Location: **Osaka, Japan**
Construction Date: **1999**

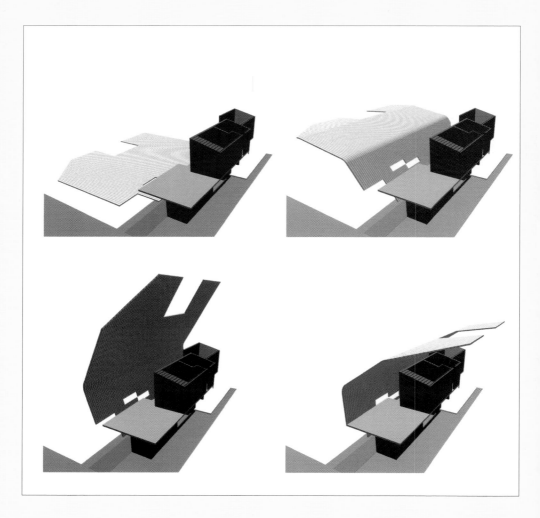

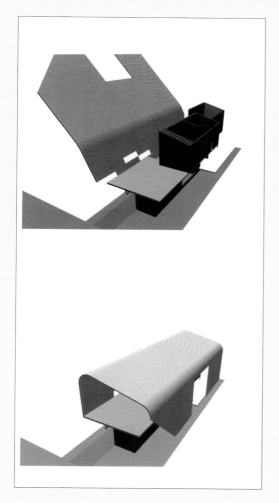

Rooftecture M is a project that suggests a chair shape for a house and workshop under construction in a small city three hours by train from Osaka.

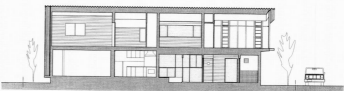

Longitudinal section

On the first floor, the rooms, including the studio, or workshop, are organized on the north front of the building, where a homogeneous illumination is ideal for working.

Inside, the rooms succeed each other independently. The interfaces between them takes up minimal space, aided by the singularity of the roof-façade skin.

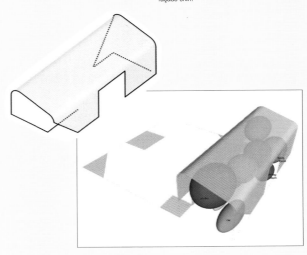

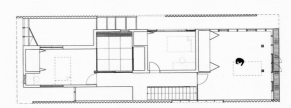

First floor plan

Ground floor plan

The Digital house

Hariri ○ Hariri. Gisue Hariri ○ Mojgan Hariri.

The house is organized around a steel frame roofed in glass that incorporates the use of a microelectronic technology of amorphous materials building up fine transparent plates into an active panel. These high-definition panels are in use by the NASA and in military aviation.

In the Digital House, the architecture involving the main bays has been cut down to simple and efficient, partially prefabricated spaces. These units come off the main structure like the spaces of an industrial building. In contrast with the three prefab bedrooms, office and school, and living room-dining room and kitchen, digitally connected to the piece, there are also transitional (circular) interspaces for people to momentarily disconnect. They thus move from virtual- to real-world tasks, contemplating their physical skills and their spiritual well-being.

This is on a nearly 2.5-acre suburban site on a slight rise and near an artificial lake. The real landscape is the low-maintenance lawn with lines of trees bordering the parterres. The virtual landscape, on the other hand, offers many possible views from the house.

The work spaces are walled in liquid crystal, replacing the individual monitors. Hence, the children's work rooms or classrooms are connected to schools all over the world, which can be followed continually.

The living room, located upstairs, is the place of entertainment and leisure. Any film or TV program is globally accessible and can be seen from a downy, organic, comfortable sofa.

Architect. Hariri ○ Hariri. Gisue Hariri ○ Mojgan Hariri.
Project sponsored by "House Beautiful"
Location: A piece of land of 2.5 acre
Construction Date: 1997○1999

This project for a studio explores the nature of domestic space in the new millennium by examining the structure of the family.

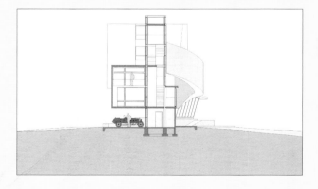

Due to the global revolution, architecture of the new millennium will have to bring into the home the activities that are going on outside of it: work, shopping, education, entertainment, and physical exercise. Within this concept, the Digital House was conceived as a prototype to examine the architecture of the new millennium.

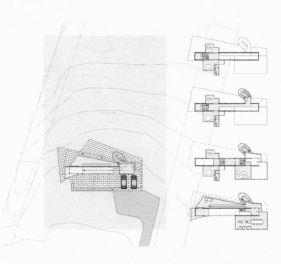